THE CRYPTOCURRENCY INVESTING BIBLE:

How to Profitably and Safely Invest in Bitcoin, Ethereum, and Other Cryptocurrencies

Jose M. Tolbert

TABLE OF CONTENT

INTRODUCTION

The emergence of cryptocurrencies has permanently changed the financial landscape in a world where change is the only constant thing. The emergence of digital assets such as Bitcoin, Ethereum, and numerous others has brought about a significant shift in our understanding of money, investments, and value itself. The Cryptocurrency Investing Bible is your go-to resource for understanding this exciting and quickly changing world. It is intended to arm you with the information and techniques needed to make profitable and secure cryptocurrency investments.

Cryptocurrencies are at the forefront of this digital financial revolution, which is continuing to revolutionize how we connect with the outside world as the digital age advances. They frequently outperform traditional investments in terms of potential for amazing financial gains. They are not without difficulties, though, as investing in cryptocurrencies can be intimidating due to the market's volatility, complicated regulations, and the frequency of fraud.

This book is meant to be your guide through the complex world of cryptocurrencies. Its goals are to reduce uncertainty, make sense of the complexities, and help you make wise decisions. The Cryptocurrency Investing Bible is your essential travel companion as you explore and grasp this new frontier in digital finance, regardless of your level of experience with investing.

This book will cover the foundations of blockchain technology, the history and significance of Ethereum and Bitcoin, and the inner workings of several different cryptocurrencies. More significantly, though, we will examine the methods and approaches that can support prudent investment management and help you make smart decisions.

To help you on this thrilling trip, these chapters contain a plethora of expert insights, useful guidance, and real-world experiences. The purpose of this book is to give you the knowledge and resources you need to make secure cryptocurrency investments. You'll get knowledge on how to safeguard your funds, spot potential ventures, and comprehend the dynamics of the market that affect the price of digital assets.

The Cryptocurrency Investing Bible will give you the information and tools you need to stay current and successfully navigate the constantly changing cryptocurrency market, from the need to do due diligence to the dangers you must avoid. This book is the key to realizing the full potential of your cryptocurrency investments, which can be safe and rewarding in the case of Bitcoin, Ethereum, and other cryptocurrencies.

This book is a vital tool for anyone looking to achieve financial independence, diversify their investment portfolio, or simply remain on top of trends. So let's start this informative adventure together, and may you have safe and prosperous cryptocurrency investments. The future of money is waiting for you here at The Cryptocurrency Investing Bible.

CHAPTER 1: THE FOUNDATION OF CRYPTOCURRENCIES

Cryptocurrencies, often known as digital or virtual currencies, are a revolutionary development in the fields of technology and finance. The blockchain is a ground-breaking idea that serves as their foundation.

Bitcoin's Origins:

The narrative starts in 2009 when a group or individual going by the alias Satoshi Nakamoto created Bitcoin. All cryptocurrencies may be traced back to Bitcoin, which established the framework for the whole industry. It was intended to be a peer-to-peer, decentralized digital currency that ran on the blockchain, a public ledger.

 Blockchain Technology's Power:

Distributed ledger technology, or blockchain, is the foundation of Bitcoin and all other cryptocurrencies. It provides a novel means of recording and verifying transactions. The blockchain is a chain of blocks, each holding a list of transactions. It is a decentralized, immutable database. Once these transactions are committed to the blockchain, they become unchangeable and permanent, safeguarded by encryption.

Key components of the blockchain are as follows:

1. Decentralized systems: The blockchain is not subject to control or manipulation by a single institution, unlike traditional financial systems that depend on central authorities such as banks and governments. Instead, the blockchain is maintained by a network of nodes.

2. Openness: Every transaction on the blockchain is visible to everyone and is publicly recorded. One of the most important components of trust in the Bitcoin world is transparency.

3. Security: Cryptographic methods make sure that a transaction is almost hard to undo or change once it is added to the blockchain.

4. Immutability: Data stored in the blockchain's history is unchangeable and permanent. A layer of dependability and trust is added by this immutability.

The Way Cryptocurrencies Work:

Based on the concepts of blockchain technology, cryptocurrencies validate and record transactions through a process called mining. This is a condensed explanation of how cryptocurrencies operate:

1.Creation of Transactions: By transferring cryptocurrency from one wallet to another, users start transactions. The network receives a broadcast of these transactions.

2. Verification and Validation: These transactions are gathered and verified by miners, which are unique nodes in the network. Together, they form a block and compete to solve a challenging mathematical challenge called, in the case of Bitcoin, Proof of Work (PoW).

3. Agreement: The new block is broadcast to the network by the first miner to solve the riddle. Once more nodes have confirmed their legitimacy, the new block is appended to the blockchain and added after a consensus is established.

4. Gift: Miners receive transaction fees and new cryptocurrency coins in exchange for their labor. They are encouraged to preserve the network and ensure its integrity as a result.

Cryptocurrencies are safe and reliable because of this consensus and mining process. It guarantees the validity of transactions and the blockchain's continued integrity as a trustworthy log of all transactions.

The blockchain, which serves as the foundation for cryptocurrencies, has not only spawned new digital currencies but also several breakthroughs and uses across a wide range of industries, including voting systems, finance, and supply chain management. Anyone wishing to buy, produce, or just use this revolutionary technology has to understand the fundamental ideas underpinning cryptocurrencies.

1:1 The Birth Of Bitcoin

In 2008, the world was still in disarray due to the ongoing global financial crisis. Amidst the economic upheaval, an enigmatic individual identified as Satoshi Nakamoto released a whitepaper entitled "Bitcoin: A Peer-to-Peer Electronic Cash System." This whitepaper established the groundwork for Bitcoin, the first cryptocurrency in history.

In this whitepaper, an unknown person or group known only as Satoshi Nakamoto offered a ground-breaking solution to the issues with conventional financial systems. The main goal was to develop a decentralized digital currency that would function without the help of governments or banks, giving people an alternative means of conducting business and storing wealth.

The following were the main factors that led to the creation of Bitcoin:

1. Decentralized systems: The goal of Bitcoin's creation was to do away with the necessity for central authorities. It enabled direct transactions between users over a peer-to-peer network of computers, or nodes. The vulnerabilities of the conventional financial systems, where banks and governments controlled a large amount of power, prompted this decentralization.

2. The use of blockchain technology The blockchain, a distributed ledger that securely and transparently records every transaction, was first proposed by Bitcoin. A network of nodes that collaborate to verify and log transactions maintained the blockchain both then and now.

3. Privilege of Digital: Because there is a 21 million coin maximum supply, Bitcoin was intended to be a deflationary currency. The idea behind this scarcity was to create an asset that would appreciate over time by mimicking some characteristics of tangible commodities like gold.

4. Proof of Work and Mining: The Proof of Work (PoW) concept served as the foundation for both the security and transaction validation procedures of Bitcoin. Miners would compete to solve challenging mathematical puzzles. Miners could be people or organizations using specialized computer hardware. Newly minted bitcoins were awarded to the first miner to answer the riddle and validate a block of transactions. In addition to securing the network, this process, called mining, created new bitcoins that were in use.

5. The use of pseudonyms The world has been captivated and intrigued by Satoshi Nakamoto's decision to stay nameless ever since. In keeping with the decentralization philosophy, this pseudonymity made sure that no one person had undue power or influence over the Bitcoin network.

Bitcoin's "genesis block," which was mined by Satoshi Nakamoto in January 2009, was the first block ever. This block included the following message embedded in it: "The Times 03/Jan/2009 Chancellor on brink of the second bailout for banks." This was a critique of the shortcomings of the established banking system as well as a nod to the financial crisis.

Technology and finance entered a new era with the introduction of Bitcoin. As a result of Bitcoin's ground-breaking architecture, dozens of different cryptocurrencies with distinctive features and functions have been developed throughout time. The influence of Bitcoin goes much beyond its use as a virtual currency; conversations concerning the direction of banking, money, and decentralized systems have resulted from it.

Since the creator(s) of Satoshi Nakamoto vanished from public view in 2010, the identity of this person remains one of the greatest mysteries of the digital era. Bitcoin is still thriving and developing today, despite its founder's obscurity, proving the strength of a decentralized, trustless financial system. With its inception, a new era marked by increased individual sovereignty over financial assets and transactions began, setting the stage for the cryptocurrency revolution.

1:2 The Formation of Ethereum

Although Bitcoin was a revolutionary first step in the realm of cryptocurrencies, the story of digital innovation didn't end there. Ethereum, sometimes regarded as the second biggest cryptocurrency, introduced a ground-breaking idea that extended beyond the realm of virtual money. With Ethereum's rise, a new chapter in blockchain and smart contract history was written.

Origin and History:

Vitalik Buterin, a young programmer and cryptocurrency enthusiast, suggested Ethereum at the end of 2013. Buterin envisioned a decentralized platform on which programmers could construct DApps (decentralized applications) and run smart contracts. Smart contracts are self-executing contracts that enable trustless transactions by doing away with the need for middlemen and having the terms of the contract directly encoded into code.

Ethereum became online in July 2015 with the release of its initial version, known as "Frontier." With this, Ethereum as a programmable, decentralized blockchain platform made its formal debut.

Important Elements and Novelties:

Ethereum differed from Bitcoin and other cryptocurrencies with the introduction of several significant features and developments, including:

1. Intelligent Contracts: The introduction of smart contracts was the most important advance made by Ethereum. Written in code, these self-executing

contracts start working automatically as soon as certain requirements are satisfied. They make it possible for a multitude of uses, including supply chain management, financial services, and even decentralized autonomous organizations (DAOs).

2. The use of decentralized apps, or DApps: With Ethereum's platform, programmers may create decentralized apps that function on the blockchain. DApps have many applications, including social networks, games, financial services, and more.

3. The Ethereum (ETH): Bitcoin is essentially a digital currency, but Ether (ETH), the native coinage of Ethereum, has two functions. Similar to Bitcoin, it can be utilized for transactions, but it also acts as "gas" to cover the cost of storage and processing on the Ethereum network.

4. the Ethereum Virtual Machine (EVM): Ethereum smart contracts may be implemented on the blockchain thanks to the EVM, a decentralized Turing-complete runtime environment. It guarantees that code runs deterministically and securely.

5. Ongoing Improvement: The growth of Ethereum is characterized by a robust and dynamic developer and contributor community. With network updates (forks), the platform keeps evolving. For example, Ethereum 2.0 switched from a Proof of Work (PoW) to a Proof of Stake (PoS) consensus method to increase scalability and energy efficiency.

Use Cases and Impact:

The blockchain and cryptocurrency space have been significantly impacted by Ethereum's rise to prominence. Numerous cutting-edge initiatives and use cases have found a home on its platform, including:

- DeFi (Decentralized Finance): The DeFi movement has been made possible by Ethereum's smart contract features, which let users engage in financial operations like lending, borrowing, and trading without the need for conventional middlemen.

-Tokens that aren't fungible (NFTs): The main platform for generating and exchanging NFTs, which have transformed the digital art, gaming, and collectibles sectors, is Ethereum.

- Autonomous organizations decentralized (DAOs): DAOs, or decentralized autonomous organizations, are run by members and regulated by code. Ethereum makes this possible, providing a new method of allocating resources and making decisions.

- Supply Chain Administration: Supply chain solutions use Ethereum's security and transparency characteristics to monitor the origin and authenticity of items.

The advent of Ethereum signifies a noteworthy turning point in the blockchain and cryptocurrency domain, as it showcased the technology's potential that extends beyond virtual currencies. Ethereum continues to be a driving force behind the creation of decentralized applications and the wider acceptance of blockchain technology, sparking a surge of creativity with its open and flexible platform. It has increased the limits of what is feasible in the digital sphere, and its effects will probably be seen for some time to come.

1:3 The Power of Blockchain Technology

With its revolutionary potential, blockchain technology—the fundamental innovation powering cryptocurrencies like Ethereum and Bitcoin—has captured the attention of people all around the world. It signifies a fundamental change in the sharing, storing, and verifying of data. The fundamental ideas of blockchain technology are what give it its power:

1.Decentralization:

Blockchain runs on what is known as a decentralized network of computers, or nodes. In contrast to conventional systems that depend on a central authority, such as a government agency or bank, blockchain transactions are verified by a dispersed network. The system is resistant to manipulation, control, and single points of failure because of its decentralization. Because there isn't a single entity with ultimate control over the blockchain, security and transparency are improved.

2. Objectivity:

On a blockchain, every transaction is entered into a public ledger that is open to public access and verification. Because it enables participants to audit and trace the history of transactions, this openness is a fundamental element that fosters responsibility and trust. It is especially important in sectors like financial services and supply chain management where trust and openness are critical.

3. Protection:

Blockchains protect data using cryptographic methods. A transaction is essentially unchangeable once it is included in a block and uploaded to the blockchain. Data integrity is ensured by the computational impossibility of tampering with previous records. Applications for this strong security include data protection and identity verification.

4. Unchangeability:

Data cannot be removed or changed once it is registered on a blockchain. This immutability is critical in fields like voting systems, real estate ownership, and contracts where maintaining the integrity of data is crucial. Establishing a permanent and verifiable history of transactions prevents fraud and disputes.

5. Lack of trust:

Participants in trustless interactions do not need to have faith in a central authority or one another thanks to blockchain technology. Consensus processes and cryptographic verification take the place of trust. Peer-to-peer transactions that are secure and eliminate the need for middlemen in a variety of industries are based on trustlessness.

6. Intelligent Contracts:

Smart contracts are self-executing contracts that have their terms encoded directly into the code. When specified circumstances are satisfied, these contracts automatically come into effect. Smart contracts simplify a variety of activities, including supply chain management and financial transactions, by doing away with the need for middlemen.

7. Digital Money:

The most well-known use of blockchain technology
is as the foundation for virtual currencies like
Ethereum and Bitcoin. These virtual currencies offer
a safe, international, and effective way to transfer
value as an alternative to conventional fiat
currencies.

8. Applications Outside of Finance:

Although the banking industry was the first to use
blockchain, there are many other possible uses for it.
Voting systems, real estate, healthcare, and supply
chain management are just a few of the sectors that
have realized how blockchain technology may
improve efficiency, security, and transparency.

9. The Token System:

Real-world assets can be represented on a
blockchain as digital tokens thanks to blockchain

technology. Tokenization has the potential to completely transform the way we trade, purchase, and sell assets by making them more efficient and accessible.

The potential of blockchain technology to upend established systems and improve their security, efficiency, and transparency is what gives it its power. It has the power to transform sectors, lower fraud rates, and boost confidence in a world going more digital. The impact that blockchain technology has on our daily lives will only grow as it develops and finds new applications.

1:4 The Mechanics of Cryptocurrencies

Blockchain technology provides the foundation for the distinct, decentralized system that underpins cryptocurrencies. Comprehending the workings of cryptocurrencies is imperative for everyone wishing to invest in, utilize, or innovate within this frontier market. This is a summary of how cryptocurrencies operate:

1. Blockchain Application:

Blockchain technology is the foundation of cryptocurrencies. A blockchain is a distributed, decentralized ledger that securely, openly, and irrevocably records every transaction. It is made up of a series of blocks, each of which has a list of transactions on it. The following are the main elements of blockchain technology:

- Decentralized systems: A global network of nodes, or computers, keeps the blockchain up to date. By doing away with the requirement for a central authority, this decentralization improves security and transparency.

- Openness: Every transaction on the blockchain is visible to everyone and is recorded. One of the most important components of trust in the Bitcoin world is transparency.

- Protection: On the blockchain, transactions and data are secured through the use of cryptographic algorithms. A transaction is practically impenetrable once it is added to the blockchain.

- Immutability: Historical data stored on the blockchain is unchangeable and permanent. The data's integrity is guaranteed by its immutability.

2. Security using Cryptography:

Cryptographic methods are essential to the security of cryptocurrencies. In this context, two crucial ideas are:

-Keys, both public and private: A public key, which serves as an address in the cryptocurrency system, and a private key, which is used to sign transactions, are owned by each user. While private keys are required to authorize transactions and must be kept secret, public keys can be used to receive cryptocurrency.

-Combination Functions: Cryptographic hash functions are used by cryptocurrencies to safeguard data and produce distinct transaction and block representations. It is challenging to change already-existing records because modifications to the input data produce completely different hash returns.

3. Exchanges

The main way that users move cryptocurrency to one another is through transactions. Usually, the procedure entails the following steps:

-Starting Point: When creating a transaction, a user needs to provide the address of the recipient, the amount to be sent, and their private key for signature.

-Confirmation: The transaction is sent out to the network, where nodes check its authenticity and accuracy. The method of verification aids in preventing double-spending, or the use of the same cryptocurrency twice.

-Incorporation into a Block: After being validated, miners (in Proof of Work systems) or validators (in Proof of Stake systems) add the transaction to a block.

- Block Confirmation: The transaction is permanently secured when the block containing it is added to the blockchain.

4. Consensus and Mining:

Miners compete to solve challenging mathematical puzzles in Proof of Work (PoW) cryptocurrencies like Bitcoin, guaranteeing the security and legitimacy of transactions. The new block is broadcast to the network by the first miner to solve the puzzle, and subsequent nodes confirm its authenticity. The block is appended to the blockchain if a consensus is achieved.

Validators are selected to produce new blocks in Proof of Stake (PoS) systems, such as Ethereum 2.0, based on the quantity of bitcoin they own and are prepared to "stake" as collateral.

5. Purses:

Users of cryptocurrencies keep their assets in digital wallets. Wallets can be hardware wallets (physical devices), software wallets (internet or mobile apps), or paper wallets (printed QR codes). Wallets, which are protected by private keys, are used to store and access cryptocurrency assets.

6. Interactions Between Peers:

Peer-to-peer transactions—in which users transfer money directly to one another without the need for middlemen—are made possible by cryptocurrencies. After being broadcast to the network, transactions are verified by nodes and stored on the blockchain. The use of banks or payment processors is eliminated by this decentralized, trustless approach.

Gaining an understanding of the workings of cryptocurrencies is essential for interacting with and profiting from the world of digital assets. This includes blockchain technology, cryptographic security, transaction processing, mining, and wallet operations. Businesses and individual users alike will find this knowledge increasingly valuable as cryptocurrencies continue to develop and acquire wider recognition.

CHAPTER 2: TYPES OF CRYPTOCURRENCIES

Since the launch of Bitcoin in 2009, cryptocurrencies have become increasingly popular. Cryptocurrencies come in thousands of varieties, each with special attributes and uses. The following are a few of the main categories of cryptocurrencies:

1. Coin (Bitcoin): Often called digital gold, Bitcoin is the first and most well-known cryptocurrency. Its main functions as a medium of exchange and a store of value are as follows. Due to its decentralized and deflationary characteristics, Bitcoin is a well-liked investment option and a hedge against inflation.

2. Use of altcoins: Any cryptocurrency that isn't Bitcoin is referred to as an altcoin. Each of the thousands of cryptocurrencies has a unique set of

applications. Litecoin (LTC), Cardano (ADA), Ethereum (ETH), and Ripple (XRP) are a few well-known examples.

3. Platforms for Smart Contracts: Developers can use these cryptocurrencies, which include Ethereum (ETH), Binance Coin (BNB), and Polkadot (DOT), to design and run smart contracts and decentralized applications (DApps). They make it possible for agreements to be programmed and self-executing, automating a variety of tasks.

4. Privacy Coins: Anonymity and confidentiality are given top priority in privacy-focused cryptocurrencies like Monero (XMR) and Zcash (ZEC). They safeguard user privacy by obscuring transaction details using cutting-edge cryptography algorithms.

5. Consistent Coins: The goal of stablecoins is to keep their value constant; they are frequently correlated with established fiat currencies like the US dollar. Some well-known examples are Tether (USDT), USD Coin (USDC), and Dai (DAI). They are frequently utilized in decentralized finance (DeFi) applications, trading, and as a refuge during market turbulence.

6. Keys to Security: Using blockchain technology, security tokens reflect real-world assets like stocks, real estate, or commodities. They offer a digital form of ownership together with possible security and liquidity advantages.

7. Tokens of Utility: Utility tokens are intended to be used on a particular platform or ecosystem. They may grant access to goods, services, or privileges inside that ecosystem. Examples are Chainlink

(LINK) for decentralized oracles and Binance Coin (BNB) for the Binance exchange.

8. NFTs: Non-Fungible Tokens: NFTs are distinct digital assets that signify possession of a certain object, work of art, or collectible. They are unique from other tokens and indivisible, which has led to their rise in prominence in the gaming and art industries.

9. DeFi Tokens: These tokens, which stand for Decentralized Finance, can be used to trade, lend, and borrow money without the use of conventional financial middlemen. Maker (MKR), Aave (AAVE), and Uniswap (UNI) are a few examples.

10. Tokens of Governance: The ability to take part in the governance and decision-making of a decentralized platform or organization is granted to token holders. In their ecosystems, Compound

(COMP) and Yearn. finance (YFI) tokens, for example, grant voting rights.

11. Cross-Chain Tokens: Cross-chain coins are designed to make it easier for various blockchain networks to communicate with one another. DOT and ATOM stand for Polkadot, two instances of blockchains that aim to be connected.

12. Environmental and Energy-Friendly Coins: To lessen their influence on the environment, several cryptocurrencies, including Chia (XCH) and Holo (HOT), concentrate on more energy-efficient consensus techniques, like proof-of-stake and proof-of-space.

It's crucial to remember that the cryptocurrency market is extremely dynamic and that new tokens and coin varieties are always being created. Every cryptocurrency has a distinct function, and there might be significant differences in their acceptance, use cases, and prices. It is essential for anyone wishing to invest, utilize, or interact with blockchain technology and the digital economy to comprehend the various kinds of cryptocurrencies.

2:1 Bitcoin: Digital Gold and Beyond

Bitcoin, also known as "digital gold," has had a profound effect on technology and the banking industries. Although its first function was as a digital currency, it has developed into much more than just a means of transaction. Let's investigate the idea that Bitcoin is "digital gold" and its wider implications.

Electronic Gold:

1. Value Store: Bitcoin's potential as a store of value gives rise to the comparison with gold. Bitcoin is viewed as a hedge against inflation and economic risks, much like gold. Due to its limited quantity of 21 million coins and deflationary issuance, it has drawn interest from investors looking for a dependable digital store of value.

2. Resource Scarcity: Bitcoin is digitally scarce, much like gold is physically scarce. It appeals to people seeking an asset that is resistant to being quickly depreciated by excessive creation because of its limited quantity.

3. World Acknowledgment: The consensus that Bitcoin is a worthwhile asset is expanding. More organizations and people are beginning to recognize it as a store of value, and its value is frequently stated alongside more conventional assets like stocks and gold.

4. Secure Haven: A safe refuge in uncertain or turbulent economic times has been thought to be Bitcoin. People use it to protect their riches, particularly in nations where there are currency limitations or devaluations.

Moving Past Digital Gold:

Even though Bitcoin is frequently compared to digital gold, its uses and potential extend beyond just being a store of value:

1. Chain of Trade: In the beginning, Bitcoin was intended to be a peer-to-peer digital currency that would facilitate safe, international transactions. Due to its extreme volatility and scalability issues, its usefulness as a medium of exchange has decreased, although it is still an alternative for some types of transactions.

2. Investment in Digital: Both institutional and individual investors are drawn to Bitcoin, which is currently recognized as an asset class for investments. It is a speculative investment and a means of diversifying portfolios.

3. Founder of Blockchain Technology: The initial success of Bitcoin has made it possible for blockchain technology to be adopted more widely. The blockchain idea, which was first popularized by Bitcoin, is currently employed in several fields outside of cryptocurrencies.

4. Champion of Innovation: Thousands of alternative cryptocurrencies and decentralized apps have been developed as a result of Bitcoin. Because of Bitcoin's pioneering position, the crypto industry is still evolving.

5. Financial Inclusion: Bitcoin can give underbanked or unbanked individuals access to financial services and the global economy.

6. Transparency and Security: A variety of industries, including voting systems, real estate, and supply chain management, rely on the security and

transparency features of Bitcoin's blockchain technology.

 Bitcoin's reputation as "digital gold" is evidence of both its growing significance in the financial industry and its ability to function as a trustworthy store of value. Its fundamental purpose as a digital currency has not changed, but it has grown to fulfill many more roles and has come to represent the larger blockchain and cryptocurrency revolution. Beyond being compared to gold, its influence extends beyond that, as it continues to spur innovation and transform our understanding of money, assets, and financial institutions.

2:2 Ethereum: The Smart Contract Platform

The world's most popular smart contract platform, Ethereum, signifies a radical change in the way we think about programmable agreements and decentralized applications. Let's examine Ethereum's function as a platform for smart contracts and its importance within the blockchain network.

Ethereum's Origins:

Vitalik Buterin first proposed Ethereum in late 2013, and the network was operational in 2015 after official development started in 2014. Buterin envisioned a platform that would be able to do sophisticated, self-executing contracts, or "smart contracts," and go beyond what Bitcoin could do. With Ethereum, the idea of a Turing-complete blockchain was presented, opening the door for developers to create a vast array of decentralized apps (DApps).

Essential Elements of Ethereum:

Among Ethereum's special qualities as a smart contract platform are:

1. Intelligent Contracts: Self-executing contracts with terms and conditions encoded in code are known as smart contracts. They run automatically when certain parameters are satisfied. Applications for this feature are numerous and include supply chain management, identity verification, gaming, and decentralized finance (DeFi).

2. The use of decentralized apps, or DApps: Developers can use Ethereum's platform to create DApps that are integrated into its blockchain. DApps can provide a wide range of features and

services, including financial services, social networks, and gaming.

3. Ethereum (ETH): While Ether (ETH), the primary cryptocurrency of Ethereum, functions as "gas" to pay for computational processes on the Ethereum network as well as a means of transaction, Bitcoin is primarily digital money.

4. the Ethereum Virtual Machine (EVM): The Ethereum blockchain enables smart contracts to be performed through the EVM, a decentralized runtime environment. It guarantees deterministic and safe code execution.

5. Ongoing Improvement: The developer and contributor community on Ethereum is robust and vibrant. To increase scalability and energy efficiency, the platform has undergone major modifications and is switching from a Proof of

Work (PoW) to a Proof of Stake (PoS) consensus mechanism with Ethereum 2.0.

Use Cases and Impact:

The blockchain and cryptocurrency industries have been greatly impacted by Ethereum's rise to prominence as a smart contract platform. It has made way for a wide range of creative initiatives and applications, such as:

- DeFi (Decentralized Finance): The DeFi movement revolves around Ethereum, which enables users to engage in financial transactions including lending, borrowing, and trading without the need for middlemen.

-Tokens that aren't fungible (NFTs): The main platform for generating and exchanging NFTs, which have transformed digital collectibles, gaming, and art, is Ethereum.

- Autonomous organizations decentralized (DAOs): Ethereum offers a new method of managing resources and decision-making by enabling the development of DAOs, or decentralized autonomous organizations run by their members and governed by code.

- Supply Chain Administration: Supply chain solutions use Ethereum's security and transparency characteristics to monitor the origin and authenticity of items.

- Identification Verification: Decentralized identification solutions that give people authority over their data can be made with Ethereum.

Beyond merely enabling smart contracts, Ethereum's function as a platform for smart contracts has sparked a wave of creativity and is propelling the creation of decentralized apps and the wider adoption of blockchain technology. Its programmability and flexibility make it a powerful and adaptable platform that will influence decentralized applications in the future as well as how we engage with digital assets and services.

2:3 Altcoins: Exploring Diverse Cryptocurrency Projects

Although thousands of alternative cryptocurrencies, also known as "altcoins," have emerged in the realm of blockchain and cryptocurrency, Bitcoin still leads the way and is the most well-known digital currency. A wide variety of features, applications, and innovations are available with these altcoins. Let's investigate the idea of altcoins and examine some of their special qualities.

What Are Alternative Coins?

"Alternative coins," or "altcoins," are any cryptocurrencies that aren't Bitcoin. They are constructed on different blockchain networks, each with special characteristics. There are several reasons why altcoins were developed, including:

1. Various Use Cases: Altcoins frequently concentrate on offering unique use cases or solutions to particular issues that Bitcoin might not be able to handle.

2. Improved Technology: Some alternative coins aim to enhance the scalability, privacy features, or transaction speed of Bitcoin.

3. Experimentation: Developers can test out novel concepts, consensus techniques, and governance frameworks on an altcoin platform.

4. Governance and Community: Altcoins frequently feature unique governance and community structures. While some are run by centralized organizations, others are driven by the community.

Types of Alternative Coins:

Although there are many different kinds of altcoins, the following can be made based on their main characteristics and application cases:

1. Privacy Coins: By utilizing cutting-edge cryptographic algorithms, privacy-focused altcoins like Monero (XMR) and Zcash (ZEC) prioritize user anonymity and secret transactions.

2. Smart Contract Platforms: Altcoins that support the creation of decentralized apps (DApps) and the execution of smart contracts include Ethereum (ETH), Binance Coin (BNB), and Cardano (ADA). They are renowned for being adaptable and programmable.

3. Constable Coins: The purpose of stablecoins, such as Tether (USDT) and USD Coin (USDC), is to keep their value constant by tying them to

conventional fiat currencies. They are frequently used for trading and as a refuge during volatile markets.

4. Utility Tokens: In certain blockchain ecosystems, users can utilize utility tokens like Chainlink (LINK) and Polkadot (DOT) to gain access to goods, services, or voting privileges.

5. Entertainment and Gaming Tokens: Virtual asset ownership and content monetization are made possible by altcoins that cater to the gaming and entertainment sectors, such as Decentraland (MANA) and Basic Attention Tokens (BAT).

6. DeFi Tokens: Lending, borrowing, and trading are just a few of the financial services made possible by Decentralized Finance (DeFi) tokens like Maker (MKR), Aave (AAVE), and Uniswap (UNI).

7. Intellectual Property (NFT): NFTs are distinct digital assets that stand in for ownership of particular objects, works of art, or collectibles. Digital art and gaming are two areas they have revolutionized.

8. Governance Tokens: Within decentralized organizations and platforms, voting rights are granted by governance tokens like Compound (COMP) and Yearn. finance (YFI).

9. Cross-Chain Tokens: Cross-chain cryptocurrencies, like Polkadot (DOT), are designed to make it easier for data and assets to flow between various blockchain networks.

10. Tokens with Low Energy Use: Certain alternative coins emphasize consensus methods that use less energy, such as proof-of-stake (PoS) or

proof-of-space. Cardano (ADA) and Chia (XCH) are two examples.

Innovation and Risk:

Although the wide variety of cryptocurrencies presents intriguing opportunities, it's critical to understand that there are differing levels of risk associated with them. Since the cryptocurrency market is so speculative, not every altcoin will be profitable. An altcoin's technology and team should be thoroughly understood by investors, and they should also take into account the project's potential adoption and real-world use case.

The cryptocurrency space is a living example of a decentralized system and blockchain experimentation. While some altcoins might bring about ground-breaking breakthroughs, others can become obscure. A vital component of remaining informed and taking part in the vibrant and ever-evolving cryptocurrency ecosystem is investigating altcoins and comprehending their distinctive qualities.

CHAPTER 3: THE CRYPTOCURRENCY MARKET

In the larger context of finance, the cryptocurrency market is a vibrant and quickly developing industry. With a diverse array of functions and applications, it includes all kinds of digital assets and tokens. The cryptocurrency market, its main elements, and its importance are summarized as follows:

Digital Resources:

1.The first cryptocurrencies To serve as a means of exchange, are virtual or digital currencies. A plethora of cryptocurrencies exist, commonly known as altcoins, while Bitcoin (BTC) is the most popular one.

2. Empty Tokens Many digital resources, utilities, or rights are represented by tokens. Decentralized ecosystems can utilize them for specific purposes and issue them on blockchain platforms. Tokens with utility, security, and non-fungible characteristics are a few examples (NFTs).

Capitalization of the Market:

The total worth of all cryptocurrencies in use is represented by market capitalization, a crucial statistic. Each cryptocurrency's current price is multiplied by its total supply to determine this. Understanding the market capitalization of several cryptocurrencies allows one to ascertain their relative sizes and levels of popularity.

Trade-ins:

An online marketplace for buying, selling, and trading digital assets is provided by cryptocurrency exchanges. Bitfinex, Binance, Coinbase, and Kraken are some of the most well-known exchanges. Users can swap one cryptocurrency for another or fiat currencies like the US dollar or euro using these platforms' diverse trading pairs.

Pocketbook:

A digital instrument called a cryptocurrency wallet is used to send, receive, and store cryptocurrency. Paper wallets (printed private keys), hardware wallets (physical devices), and software wallets (internet or mobile apps) are the three types of wallets. For managing digital assets, they offer a secure solution.

Diurnal swings:

The market volatility of cryptocurrencies is well-known. For traders and investors, there are possibilities and hazards associated with the sudden and dramatic variations in prices. Market sentiment, current affairs, legislative changes, and speculative trading are some of the factors that cause volatility.

Guideline:

Different countries and regions have different cryptocurrency regulations. Cryptocurrencies are accepted in some nations while they are strictly regulated or completely prohibited in others. Market and investor confidence are susceptible to substantial effects from regulatory changes.

Applications:

Blockchain technology and cryptocurrencies are useful in many different contexts.

-Digital Currency: Enabling peer-to-peer exchanges devoid of middlemen.

- Smart Contracts: Self-executing contracts with code-based conditions.

-Decentralized Finance (DeFi): provided Financing services like lending, borrowing, and trading.

Non-Fungible Tokens (NFTs): stand for distinct digital assets and collectibles.

Supply Chain Management: Monitoring the origin and legitimacy of items.
Securing and decentralizing identification solutions through the provision of identity verification services.

Video Games and Virtual Assets: Including digital assets into virtual worlds and video games.

Investment and Conjecture :

Cryptocurrencies are seen as an investment asset class by many people and organizations. In the hopes of seeing a rise in value over time, they acquire and hold digital assets. Additionally, speculative traders interested in making money on transient price swings have been drawn to the cryptocurrency market.

Innovative Approaches and Difficulties:

New initiatives and innovations are often coming up in the Bitcoin business, which is known for its continual innovation. Regulating uncertainty, scalability issues, and security concerns are some of the other difficulties it faces. Continued growth and adaptation are necessary to meet these difficulties.

 the worlds of technology and finance are being fundamentally changed by the bitcoin industry. It provides a myriad of digital materials with a variety of applications and room for creativity. If one wants to be involved in this vibrant and quickly changing industry, one must have a solid understanding of its components and dynamics.

3:1 Market Volatility: Friend or Foe?

Market volatility, which is a gauge of price swings, is a key feature of both the cryptocurrency and wider financial markets. Depending on your point of view and investing approach, it may be a friend or an enemy. Let's examine both viewpoints:

Friend: Possibilities for Profit

1. Profitability: Profitable trading and investing opportunities are generated by volatility. Price swings make it possible to purchase low and sell high, which can result in significant profits, particularly for investors who are knowledgeable about technical analysis and market patterns.

2. Observing Day Trading: Volatility in the market might be advantageous to active traders. Day traders

profit from volatility by making fast trades to take advantage of slight price differences. They live on short-term price swings.

3. diversification Traditional investing portfolios can benefit from diversification in volatile markets. Including assets with minimal correlation to traditional assets, such as cryptocurrency, may help lower the overall risk of the portfolio.

4. Creativity: Adoption and innovation eras are sometimes accompanied by volatility. For example, cryptocurrencies have seen a great deal of price volatility even as they have fueled new use cases for decentralized banking and blockchain technology.

Foe: Uncertainty and Risk

1. Defeats: Market volatility carries a danger of large losses in addition to the potential for gains.

When prices fall as fast as they rise, people who are unprepared for market fluctuations may suffer significant financial losses.

2. The Stress of Emotions: Market volatility can be emotionally taxing. Price changes have the potential to cause fear and worry, which can lead to rash judgments. Trading based on emotions frequently ends in losses.

3. Imprudence: Excessive volatility can breed uncertainty, which makes it difficult to forecast market changes and make wise investment choices. Price changes can be unpredictable and driven by news events, market sentiment, and other forces.

4. Risk to Regulation: Price movements in the cryptocurrency market can be significantly impacted by changes in regulations. Investors may be exposed

to more risk due to unpredictability surrounding future laws.

Managing Volatility:

Market volatility can be a friend or a foe, depending on your approach, goals, and risk tolerance. The following are some efficient methods for handling volatility:

1. Diversification: Spreading your risk can be achieved by distributing your investing portfolio over several asset classes rather than concentrating all of your money on one coin.

2. Length of Time View: The emotional impact of short-term price changes can be lessened by adopting a long-term perspective. Investors who have faith in an asset's underlying value could be less impacted by daily price fluctuations.

3. Risk Management: Put risk management techniques into practice, such as placing stop-loss orders or reducing the amount of your portfolio that is invested in high-risk stocks.

4. Studies and Instruction: An informed investor is more capable of making wise choices. Recognize the assets you invest in and keep up with market changes.

5. Self-Control in Emotions: Remain emotionally composed. Refrain from acting rashly out of greed or fear. Adhere to your investment strategy.

depending on how it is handled, market volatility in the financial and cryptocurrency markets may be both a friend and a foe. Although there are financial opportunities, there are also risks and difficulties. Effectively managing market volatility requires knowing your risk tolerance, having a clear investing strategy, and engaging in disciplined risk management.

3:2 The Role of Market Exchanges

In the realm of finance, and particularly in the trade of assets such as stocks, bonds, commodities, and cryptocurrencies, market exchanges are essential. These exchanges offer a controlled marketplace where traders of different financial products can transact. An outline of the principal roles and functions of market exchanges is provided below:

1. Cost Estimation:

The primary locations for price discovery are market exchanges. By continuously matching buy and sell orders, they establish the market values of assets. These prices serve as a benchmark for asset valuation and represent the opinion and collective expertise of market players.

2. Provision of Liquidity:

Exchanges improve the financial markets' liquidity. The ease with which an asset can be purchased or sold without materially altering its price is known as liquidity. By bringing buyers and sellers together, exchanges facilitate the entry and exit of investments for investors.

3. Equitable and Open Trading:

Market exchanges enforce laws and policies that encourage moral conduct, which guarantees honest and open trade. These regulations cover transaction reporting, order execution protocols, and price and volume data openness.

4. Consolidated Market Place:

Through exchanges, a centralized marketplace is created where buyers and sellers can communicate. This centralization lowers counterparty risk, expedites trade, and gives participants a safe environment.

5. Listing of Assets:

Exchanges make it easier for different financial instruments to be listed, enabling governments to issue bonds, businesses to obtain cash through initial public offers (IPOs), and traders to transact in a variety of assets, such as stocks, commodities, and cryptocurrencies.

6. Monitoring the Market:

Exchanges use market surveillance to keep an eye on trade activity, spot odd trends or manipulation, and make sure regulations are being followed.

Investor confidence and market integrity are preserved in this way.

7. Hazard Assessment:

Exchanges frequently use risk management techniques to stop abrupt fluctuations in pricing. For example, to prevent market crashes, circuit breakers can momentarily stop trading if prices show high volatility.

8. Clearing and Settlement:

To guarantee the final and secure transfer of assets between buyers and sellers, exchanges offer clearing and settlement services. By using this procedure, counterparty risk is removed and trade integrity is guaranteed.

9. Adherence to Regulations:

To preserve investor protection and market integrity, exchanges are required to abide by regulatory rules set forth by governmental bodies. To achieve compliance, they frequently collaborate closely with regulatory agencies.

10. Segmenting the market:

To accommodate diverse asset classes, trading tactics, and investor preferences, numerous exchanges divide their markets into multiple divisions. Primary markets (for new issuances) and secondary markets (for trading existing assets) can be included in this categorization.

11. Creativity:

The financial industry's centers of innovation are exchanges. They consistently implement novel trading technologies, merchandise, and services to cater to the changing requirements of market players.

12. Worldwide Networking:

Exchanges offer worldwide connections in an increasingly linked society, enabling investors to transact in assets from all over the world. This worldwide reach increases diversification and investment options.

13. Availability:

A vast spectrum of investors can use exchanges, ranging from small-scale individual traders using online brokerage accounts to huge institutional investors and fund managers.

Specialized exchanges exist for several asset classes, including stocks, bonds, commodities, and cryptocurrencies, to meet their specific needs and legal requirements. As an essential part of the global financial ecosystem, each exchange makes it possible for assets to be traded and money to be allocated effectively.

3:3 Market Liquidity and Trading Pairs

Key ideas in the domain of financial markets and cryptocurrency exchanges include market liquidity and trading pairings. Anyone involved in asset trading, including traders and investors, must comprehend these ideas. Let's examine what trading pairs are and how the market is liquid:

Markets liquidity:

Market liquidity is the degree to which an asset's price can be changed little by buying or selling it. It gauges the level of activity and the accessibility of market players ready to exchange an item. A market with high liquidity is one in which there are many buyers and sellers, which facilitates the entry or exit of positions with little effect on the price of the asset. Conversely, low liquidity indicates fewer participants, which increases the possibility of significant price swings as a result of trading.

Among the major elements influencing market liquidity are:

1. Volatility of Trade: Since high trade volume indicates more active engagement in the market, it frequently coincides with increased liquidity.

2. Disperse: The difference between the lowest price a seller is ready to accept (the ask) and the greatest price a buyer is willing to pay (the bid) is known as the spread. Higher liquidity is typically indicated by narrow spreads.

3. Market Depth (Order Book): All of the active buy and sell orders at all price points are displayed in the order book. Stronger liquidity is indicated by a deep order book with numerous buy and sell orders.

4.Asset Market Makers: Market makers are those who provide liquidity to make trading easier. They quote buy and sell prices all the time.

5. News and Events: Outside variables, such as news stories, can affect market mood and, in turn, liquidity. Important news has the power to pull in new traders or drive existing ones out of the market.

6. Hour of Trading: Throughout the day, liquidity can change; there is typically more activity in trading during regular market hours and less during off-hours.

Trading pairs

Trading pairs are the two assets that can be exchanged against one another on cryptocurrency exchanges. For instance, Bitcoin (BTC) is traded against the US dollar (USD) in a trading pair. Because they allow users to swap one cryptocurrency for another or fiat money for another, trading pairs are crucial to cryptocurrency exchanges.

Here are some essential details regarding trading pairs:

1. Value of Base and Quotation: The base currency and the quote currency are the two assets in a trading pair. The asset you are buying or selling is denominated in base currency, and the currency you use to conduct the transaction is known as the quote currency.

2. Quotation for Price: The amount of the quote currency required to buy one unit of the base currency is the exchange rate for the trading pair.

For instance, one Bitcoin is worth $50,000 if the BTC/USD exchange rate is $50,000.

3. Trading Activity: Different trading pairs have varying levels of liquidity. More popular pairs than less well-known ones typically have more liquidity, such as BTC/USD and ETH/USD.

4. Middle Pairs: There are trading pairs available on certain exchanges that do not use fiat money. These are called cross pairs, like XRP/LTC (Ripple to Litecoin) or BTC/ETH (Bitcoin to Ethereum).

5. Discrepancy: By taking advantage of price disparities across other exchanges for the same trading pair, traders sometimes participate in arbitrage. The fact that trading pairs are available on several platforms makes this method easier to implement.

To make wise selections, traders and investors need to understand trading pairs and market liquidity. The choice of trading pairs enables people to diversify their holdings and take advantage of a range of investment opportunities in the realm of cryptocurrencies and financial markets, while liquidity affects how simple it is to purchase and sell.

CHAPTER 4: BUILDING YOUR CRYPTOCURRENCY INVESTMENT PORTFOLIO

Building an investing portfolio for cryptocurrencies is a calculated risk that requires careful preparation, diversification, and management. Here are some steps to think about when assembling your portfolio, regardless of experience level with cryptocurrencies:

1. Research and Education:

It's crucial to educate oneself about the market, specific assets, and blockchain technology before you begin investing in cryptocurrencies. Here are a few crucial actions:

- Gain knowledge of several cryptocurrencies, their applications, and related technologies.
- Recognize the dangers of investing in cryptocurrencies, such as market volatility and shifting regulations.
. Keep up with news and changes in the cryptocurrency field.

2. Establish Your Investment Objectives:

Establish your risk tolerance and investing objectives:

- Do you want to focus on long-term development, short-term rewards, or both?
. Determine the amount of risk you can bear and the amount of money you are willing to invest.
. Think about your time range and financial objectives.

3. Spread Out Your Assets:

One essential tactic for risk management is diversification. Refrain from investing all of your money in a single cryptocurrency. To lower risk, disperse your investments among several assets. Think about a variety of cryptocurrency kinds, including well-known coins like Ethereum and Bitcoin and emerging altcoins.

4. Choosing Assets:

Make asset selections depending on your objectives and study. Several things to think about are:

- Market liquidity and capitalization.
Technology and application.
- Community and development team help.
- Past results and trends in prices.

5. Hazard Assessment:

Put risk management techniques into practice to safeguard your investments:

To reduce possible losses, place stop-loss orders. Spend only money you can afford to lose.
- Spread out your holdings to reduce risk.
- For safe storage, think about utilizing hardware wallets.

6. Continue to Learn:

The marketplaces for cryptocurrencies are very active. Stay up to date with:

Staying up to date on industry news and updates.
- Keeping an eye on your portfolio and making any adjustments.

- Remaining up to date on local regulatory developments.

7. Protection:

A key consideration in the Bitcoin world is security. Employ safe procedures such as:

Employing trustworthy exchanges and wallets.
- Setting up your accounts to use two-factor authentication (2FA).
- Preserving your keys.

8. A Long-Term View:

Investing in cryptocurrencies can be very risky. Keeping an eye on the big picture and considering how the technology will affect future developments might help you make better decisions in the long run.

9. Tax-Related Issues:

Recognize the tax ramifications of your bitcoin holdings. Trading cryptocurrencies might result in capital gains taxes in some areas, so you might need to notify the tax authorities of your transactions.

10. Get Expert Counsel:

If you are unsure about the investments you are making, think about speaking with a tax expert or financial counselor who specializes in cryptocurrency.

Recall that there are dangers associated with cryptocurrency investing and no assurances of profit. To create a cryptocurrency investment portfolio that fits your financial objectives and risk tolerance, it's critical to make educated judgments, stay informed, and adopt a balanced strategy.

4:1 The Art of Diversification

One of the most important investment strategies is diversification, which means distributing your money over a variety of assets to lower risk and increase the likelihood of steady returns. This idea holds for many different financial markets, such as bonds, equities, and cryptocurrency markets. Developing a balanced investment portfolio and managing risk can be accomplished using the skill of diversification. ideas to think about:

1. Distributed Throughout Asset Classes:

Spread your money throughout a variety of asset classes, including:

- Investments: This includes stocks or company shares, which have a higher risk but may offer growth potential.

- Fixed Income: If you want a more steady and predictable income, consider investing in bonds or other debt instruments.

- Real Assets: Take into account commodities, real estate, or items with inherent value, such as gold.

- Digital Money: Add ethereal investments to your portfolio, such as altcoins and Bitcoin, which can expand and diversify.

The risk resulting from market volatility in any one asset class can be reduced by diversifying across asset classes.

2. Distribute according to Risk Tolerance:

Your allocation ought to be in line with your financial objectives and risk tolerance. A higher portion of your portfolio may be devoted to safe assets like cash or bonds if you have a low tolerance for risk. You might invest more in growth assets like stocks and cryptocurrencies if you have a higher risk tolerance.

3. Diversification by Region:

Take into account purchasing assets from various geographic locations. This can shield your portfolio from geopolitical crises and economic downturns that are peculiar to a given region.

4. Industry and Sector Diversification:

Diversify among several industries or sectors within each asset class. Invest in businesses from a variety of industries, such as technology, healthcare, and finance, when investing in the stock market. This lessens the risk brought on by difficulties unique to a given industry.

5. Horizon of Time:

One of the most important factors in diversification is your investment time horizon. You might be able to assume greater risk and dedicate a larger portion of your portfolio to investments with better growth potential if you have a long-term outlook. More conservative investments may be preferred by short-term investors.

6. Adjust Portfolio Balance:

Verify and adjust your portfolio regularly to make sure it is in line with your goals. You may notice a change in the allocation of your portfolio from its initial balance when certain assets perform extraordinarily well or poorly. Rebalancing is the process of acquiring or disposing of assets to keep your intended asset allocation.

7. Take Into Account Unrelated Assets:

Select assets with minimal links to one another. This indicates that they don't usually move simultaneously in the same direction. For instance, during market swings, equities and bonds frequently exhibit a negative correlation, which qualifies them for diversification.

8. The Risk-Return Balance:

Recall that risk cannot be eliminated by diversity. Rather, it distributes and controls risk. It's critical to strike a balance between the risk and return potential

of various investments to achieve your financial
objectives.

One tactic to help control risk and strengthen the
stability of your investing portfolio is
diversification. Instead of attempting to predict
winners every time, you should aim to build a well-
rounded portfolio of assets that will enable you to
weather market turbulence and advance toward your
financial goals.

4:2 Assessing Risk Tolerance

Assessing your level of risk tolerance is an essential first step in creating an investing strategy that complements your personality and financial objectives. Your level of comfort with the possibility of losing money in exchange for a chance to make money is reflected in your risk tolerance. The following elements and things to think about can help you determine your risk tolerance:

1. Budgetary Objectives:

Think about your long- and short-term financial goals. These objectives should be in line with your risk tolerance. For instance:

- A reduced risk tolerance and a preference for investments like bonds or dividend stocks may be more appropriate if your main objectives are capital preservation or income production.

If building wealth over the long term is your goal and you can live with temporary swings, you might be more willing to take on risk and allocate more of your investment portfolio to equities and cryptocurrency.

2. Duration of Investment:

Your risk tolerance is mostly determined by the length of time you have invested:

- You might be more tolerant of short-term market volatility if you have a long investment horizon.

Short-term objectives, like purchasing a home within the next few years, can call for safer, more reliable assets.

3. Financial Circumstances:

Examine your income, expenses, savings, emergency fund, and overall financial status right now. You may be able to choose your investments and risk tolerance more freely if you have a solid financial base.

4. Risk Acceptance:

The capability to bear financial losses without adversely affecting your lifestyle or financial stability is known as your risk capacity. Your ability to take risks is influenced by things like your income, savings, and job stability.

5. Personality and Emotion:

Think about how you feel about taking on financial risk. Does market volatility make you feel at ease, or does it make you stressed and anxious? Determining your risk tolerance might be aided by understanding your emotional responses.

6. Expertise and Understanding:

Your risk tolerance may be influenced by your degree of investment experience as well as your understanding of financial markets and asset classes. More seasoned investors may generally be more willing to take on risk.

7. Blending in:

Because diversification distributes investments among a variety of assets, it can help reduce risk. A more balanced risk-return profile can be obtained with a diversified portfolio.

8. Tools for Risk Assessment:

Financial organizations and investment platforms offer a variety of risk assessment tools and surveys. These tools help you determine your risk tolerance by asking you questions about your goals, financial status, and preferred level of risk.

9. Speak with an advisor on finances:

See a financial advisor if you're unclear about your risk tolerance or if you require expert advice. They may assist in determining your risk tolerance and financial status, suggest suitable investing techniques, and build a diversified portfolio that supports your objectives.

As your financial status and aspirations change, it's important to routinely reevaluate your risk tolerance because it can alter over time. Your investing choices should be guided by your risk tolerance, which will also assist you in building a portfolio that strikes a balance between your comfort level with probable losses and your desire for profits.

4:3 Strategies for Long-Term and Short-Term Investments

Your time horizon, risk tolerance, and financial objectives can all influence your choice of investment techniques. The following techniques are suited for both short-term and long-term investments:

Investments Over Long Term:

Usually, long-term investments are kept for several years or even decades. They frequently prioritize accumulating wealth and ensuring financial stability. The following are some long-term investing strategies:

1. Investing in the stock market: A large percentage of the portfolios of long-term investors is frequently

allocated to equities. Stocks have historically demonstrated a high potential for long-term growth. To spread the risk, diversify your stock holdings.

2. Titles: Bonds can generate a consistent revenue source and are generally stable. Bonds should make up a chunk of your portfolio, particularly if you are risk-averse.

3. diversification of a diversified portfolio can lower risk. Your long-term portfolio should include a variety of asset classes, including foreign assets, commodities, and real estate.

4. Buy and Hold: Invest in reliable assets and hang onto them for years, despite brief market swings, by using a "buy and hold" strategy.

5. Average Dollar Cost: Regardless of the state of the market, invest a set amount of money regularly

(such as monthly). This tactic can assist in lessening the effects of market volatility.

6. Retirement Accounts: To save for retirement, make use of tax-advantaged retirement accounts such as 401(k)s and IRAs.

7. Reinvest Dividends: To take advantage of compound returns, reinvest dividends and interest received from your assets.

8. Regular Review: Make sure your long-term investments are in line with your objectives and risk tolerance by reviewing them regularly and making any necessary adjustments.

Quick-Pay Out Investments:

The goal of short-term investments is liquidity and comparatively fast profits. Usually, they are retained for a few days, weeks, or even years. The following are some short-term investing strategies:

1. Money and Its Convertibles: Keep some cash or cash equivalents, such as money market funds, as part of your portfolio. These make money easily accessible for unforeseen expenses.

2. Accounts with High Yields: Invest your money in certificates of deposit (CDs) or high-yield savings accounts for higher returns than standard savings accounts.

3. Status of Fixed Income: Compared to equities, short-term bonds and Treasury bills (T-bills) are less volatile and can yield a steady income.

4. Technical Analysis and Trading: Technical analysis is a common tool used by short-term traders

to spot short-term market movements and make fast transactions.

5. Arbitrage: Seek out chances to profit from price discrepancies in the same item across many exchanges.

6. Attribution: Leverage multiplies both gains and losses, so use it with caution. Leverage is occasionally used by short-term traders to boost returns, although it carries a higher risk.

7. Orders to Stop Losing: Put stop-loss orders into place to reduce possible losses on ephemeral deals. This is a tool for risk management.

8. Notes and Happenings: Keep abreast of news and happenings that may have an impact on transient price changes and trading opportunities.

9. Risk Management: Clarify your entry and exit points for short-term transactions and define your risk tolerance. Refrain from making snap decisions.

Keep in mind that due to increased volatility and the possibility of experiencing rapid losses, short-term investing can be riskier than long-term investing. For short-term investments, having a clear strategy and risk management plan is essential. When trading frequently, take taxes, fees, and transaction expenses into account as well.

CHAPTER 5: CONDUCTING DUE DILIGENCE

When thinking about investing or making financial decisions, due diligence is an essential step in the process. To make wise decisions, it entails investigating, dissecting, and assessing a variety of investment-related factors. Regardless of the asset you're investing in—stocks, real estate, cryptocurrency, or anything else—due diligence can help you reduce risks and increase the possibility of profitable ventures. Here's how to properly perform due diligence:

1. Establish Your Investment Objectives:

Make sure you understand your investment goals before you begin your due research. Are you aiming for income creation, wealth preservation, capital appreciation, or any mix of these? Knowing your objectives will enable you to concentrate on the appropriate kinds of investments.

2. Examine Your Investment:

Become knowledgeable about the particular investment you are thinking of making. Depending on the asset class, this could entail:

Stocks: Examine the company's balance sheet, future growth potential, competitive landscape, and market trends. Examine the company's news, earnings reports, and financial statements.

A Real Property: Analyze the location, state, market trends, potential for rental income, and estimated maintenance expenses of the property. Examine the area, real estate prices, and demand for rentals.

Digital Money: Examine the cryptocurrency's technology, use case, development team, market trends, and level of community support. Recognize the hazards and the underlying blockchain technology.

3. Evaluation of Risk:

Evaluate the risks connected to the investment:

Value Hazard: Think about the volatility of the asset's price in the past and the possibility of future swings. How will the state of the market affect your investment?

Project or Company Risk: Consider the issuer's competitive advantages, management team, and financial stability before investing in stocks or cryptocurrency. Examine the technology of the project and its likelihood of being adopted in the cryptocurrency space.

Legal and Regulatory Risk: Recognize the regulatory landscape in which your venture is situated. Modifications to regulations may have a big effect.

4. Financial Evaluation:

Analyze finances according to the kind of investment:

 Stocks: Examine the cash flow, debt levels, earnings, sales growth, and financial statements. Evaluate price-to-earnings (P/E) ratios and other valuation indicators.

A Real Property: Compute the prospective rental revenue, costs, and ROI (return on investment).

Take mortgage rates and financing choices into account.

Digital Money: Examine variables such as trading volume, price history, market capitalization, and technical advancements. Analyze tokenomics and adoption prospects.

5. Comparing Markets:

Examine other investments in the same asset class that you may consider making. When evaluating equities, contrast them with industry counterparts. When evaluating real estate, contrast it with nearby comparable homes. Compare cryptocurrency to substitutes that have comparable applications.

6. Horizon of Investment:

Take your investing horizon into account. Do you want long-term growth or just short-term gains? Your investing horizon may determine which assets are better suited.

7. Legal and Tax Aspects to Be Considered:

Recognize the financial and legal ramifications of your investment. If required, seek advice from tax and legal experts, particularly for complicated investments.

8. Get Expert Counsel:

See a financial advisor or an authority on the particular asset class you're interested in if you have questions regarding your due diligence procedure or require advice.

Performing due diligence is a continuous process, so it's critical to keep up to date and analyze your investments regularly. You can improve your chances of reaching your financial objectives and make well-informed investing selections by carrying out extensive due research.

5:1 Evaluating Cryptocurrency Projects

It is essential to assess Bitcoin initiatives before purchasing any kind of digital asset. There are many different projects in the cryptocurrency world, each with its own special features, applications, and chances of success. When assessing cryptocurrency initiatives, take into account the following important factors:

1. Collaboration and Growth:

Group for Development: Analyze the development team for the project. Do they possess relevant experience and a solid foundation in blockchain technology? Examine their prior endeavors and contributions to the cryptocurrency field.

Openness: Analyze the group's openness and community relations efforts. Do they participate in community forums and social media? Do they send out project updates regularly?

Open Source: Check to see if the project's code is available for auditing and peer review.

2. Use Case and Technology:

Technological aspects: Recognize the cryptocurrency's fundamental architecture and technologies. Does it run on a reliable and secure blockchain? Does it make use of cutting-edge technology?

Use Case: Determine the main use for cryptocurrencies. Does it offer value or solve an issue in the actual world? Think about the use case's adoption potential.

3. Roadmap and White paper:

Research paper: To learn more about the project's plans, technology, and ambitions, see the whitepaper. Seek out an understandable and thorough document.

Outline: Examine the project's roadmap to find out how it intends to accomplish its objectives and benchmarks. A clear, attainable road map is necessary.

4. Adoption and Community:

Partnership Support: A project's potential may be indicated by a robust and involved community. Keep an eye on social media, community forums, and sentiment in the community.

Selection: Seek for alliances, group projects, or actual cryptocurrency acceptance. Adoption by companies or other initiatives may indicate progress.

5. Tokenomics:

Token Supply: Recognize the distribution and total supply of tokens. It is possible to thwart centralization and manipulation via a distributed token supply.

Rewards: Examine the benefits of owning or utilizing cryptocurrencies. Does any governance or stake procedures encourage sustained participation?

6. Protection:

Security Measures: Evaluate the project's security measures, including how it handles fraud, hacking, and vulnerability protection.

Inspections:Check to see if outside security audits have been performed on the project. Projects with audits are frequently regarded as more reliable.

7. The State of the Market:

Market Capitalization: Take into account the market capitalization of the project. Increased market capitalization could suggest increased uptake and steadiness.

Trading Volume: Assess the volume of trading. Increased trade volume frequently denotes market interest and liquidity.

History of Prices: Examine the cryptocurrency's past price performance. Analyze possible patterns and price trends.

8. Adherence to Regulations:

Regulating Situation: Evaluate the project's operating environment about regulations. Adherence to regional statutes and ordinances is crucial.

Regulatory or SEC Actions: As these may affect the project's future, find out if it has been the subject of any regulatory actions or inquiries.

9. Collaborations and Integrated Systems:

Partnerships: Examine any strategic alliances you may have with other businesses, groups, or websites. Collaboration can improve the project's legitimacy.

Integrations: Take into account if the cryptocurrency can be included in other projects or utilized in a variety of applications.

10. Obstacles and Difficulties:

Risks: Determine the possible dangers and difficulties the enterprise might encounter. These could be barriers relating to technology, competition, or regulations.

Competition: Assess the level of competition. Are there any other cryptocurrencies with comparable objectives, and how does this one stand out?

When assessing cryptocurrency ventures, extensive study and due diligence are crucial. Examine the technology, team, use case, and community support for the project in detail. Take into account the risk factors and any prospective difficulties as well. Make sure to diversify your holdings rather than investing all of your money in one cryptocurrency.

5:2 Identifying Red Flags and Scams

There have been several frauds and fraudulent activities in the cryptocurrency world. It's critical to recognize warning signs and possible frauds to safeguard your finances. The following are some red flags to look out for:

1. Unrealistic Return Promises:

High Returns Promised: An investment should raise serious concerns if it offers unusually high or guaranteed returns with little to no risk. There is always risk involved with legitimate investments, and profits are never assured.

2. A lack of openness:

Unidentified Group: Projects with an anonymous or unidentified development team may raise red flags. A genuine initiative ought to have an open crew whose names can be independently confirmed.

Crypt Hidden Code: A project's openness and reliability are called into question if its source code is not available for public inspection.

3. Pump and Dump Programs:

Marketing and Hype: When making investments that are strongly marketed as urgent, use caution. To lure gullible investors, scammers frequently fabricate buzz before manipulating pricing and "dumping" their assets.

4. Scams and Ponzi:

Ensured Earnings: Ponzi schemes use the money of newer investors to pay early investors large profits. Late investors lose money when the scheme fails.

5. Noncompliance with regulations:

Offered Without Registration: Verify that the investment conforms with applicable securities laws and regulations. Unregistered securities may indicate fraudulent activity.

6. Dubious Trades:

Uncontrolled Trade: Use caution when utilizing unregulated bitcoin exchanges. Remain on reputable, regulated platforms.

7. Hacking and Phishing:

Attempts at Phishing: Be cautious of phishing emails and websites that attempt to obtain your private keys or login credentials.

Unsafe Digital Wallets: Be cautious when using online wallets or services that request your private keys, and make sure your wallets are safe.

8. False Celebrities and Social Media Accounts:

Concealed Accounts: To advertise fraudulent enterprises, con artists may fabricate social media identities or adopt celebrity personas.

Always Confirm: Always look for the official website or contact details and confirm the legitimacy of social media accounts.

9. Insufficient Details:

Discernible Whitepapers: A project's whitepaper with insufficient or ambiguous information may be a sign of its validity or lack of transparency.

Illustrative Use Case: If a project doesn't provide a clear explanation of its use case or how it plans to address real-world issues, proceed with caution.

10. The Need to Make Quick Investments:

Severity: Scammers may use strategies like "limited-time offers" or threats of missing out if you don't act right away to get you to invest right away.

11. Unachievable Tokenomics:

Excessive quantity: Projects having an excessive total quantity of tokens should be avoided as this may cause value to be diluted.

Tokens Pre-Mined: A large amount of tokens held by developers may be manipulated in price.

12. Insufficient Interaction:

Inactive Progress: It may be cause for concern if the project team doesn't communicate or provide updates.

13. Lack of a clear exit plan:

No Unambiguous Exit: A project may be cause for concern if it does not clearly define how funding will be used or an exit strategy.

14. Unverified Allegations:

Unverifiable Partnerships: Check if partnerships or integrations with other projects or businesses are legitimate.

15. Lack of Responsibility:

No Consequences: There is frequently little accountability for scams, and if something goes wrong, there is no legal redress.

16. Follow Your Intuition:

-Presence: When something seems too good to be true or makes you question its veracity, follow your gut and undertake more investigation.

It is imperative to be cautious and skeptical when it comes to the cryptocurrency field. Do your homework, double-check facts, and get advice from reliable sources at all times. To safeguard other members of the cryptocurrency community, report any scams or fraudulent schemes you become aware of to the appropriate authorities or regulatory agencies.

5:3 Assessing Team, Technology, and Community

A cryptocurrency project's staff, technology, and community support should all be considered while evaluating it. These elements are crucial to the project's legitimacy and success. Here's how to assess every one of these elements:

1. Group:

A. Background and Experience of the Team

Members of the team: Examine the team members of the project, taking note of their backgrounds, responsibilities, and roles. Search for their social media and professional account links and profiles.

Pertinent Work Experience: Determine whether team members have relevant backgrounds in the project's field, cryptocurrencies, or blockchain technology. Positives include prior accomplishments and industry experience.

Openness: It's critical that team identities and backgrounds be transparent. Unverifiable names or anonymous teams may raise red flags.

B. Advisors and Development Team

Development Team: Assess the technical proficiency of the development team. Evaluate their capacity to meet the technological goals of the project.

Guardians: Verify whether the project has partnerships or trustworthy advisors who can provide legitimacy and direction.

C. Information Sharing and Updates

Continuous Updates: The team behind a project should report on its development and progress regularly. Being in constant contact with the community is a good thing.

Analysis of Responses to Questions: Assess the team's handling of queries and issues brought up by the community. Being responsive is crucial.

2. Technological:

A. Technology of Blockchain

Type of Blockchain: Identify the blockchain technology that the project is based on. Is it a private, permissioned blockchain or a public, permissionless one, similar to Ethereum or Bitcoin?

Public blockchains are typically more transparent and decentralized.

Method of Consensus: Recognize the type of consensus method being utilized, such as Proof of Stake (PoS) or Proof of Work (PoW). The implications of various techniques for decentralization and security vary.

B. Roadmap and White Paper

Research paper: To learn more about the project's plans, technology, and ambitions, see the whitepaper. Look for a document that explains the technical details and project vision straightforwardly and completely.

Outline: Examine the project's roadmap to find out how it intends to accomplish its objectives and benchmarks. A clear, attainable road map is necessary.

C. Security and Code

Get the Source Code: Determine whether the project's code is open source so that audits and peer reviews are possible. Code transparency is a good thing.

Security Measures: Examine the project's security protocols and methods for thwarting fraud, vulnerabilities, and hacking.

3. Society:

A. Participation in Community

Forums in the Community: Keep an eye on the online communities, social media accounts, and community forums for the project. A community that is engaged and active is a good thing.

Sentiment: Assess the mood of the community. Is the initiative receiving generally favorable feedback from the community, or are there worries and criticisms?

Governance: If applicable, comprehend how the project incorporates community members in development and governance initiatives.

C. Partnerships and Adoption

Adoption in Real Life: Look for indications that the cryptocurrency is being adopted or used in the real world, such as alliances with companies or organizations.

Partnerships: Examine strategic alliances with other businesses, groups, or online venues. Collaboration can improve the project's legitimacy.

C. Objectivity

Transparency: Take into account the project's level of transparency on its advancement, finances, and decision-making procedures. A transparent initiative fosters community trust.

Updates and Communication: Evaluate how often and how well the project updates the community and communicates with them.

A crucial component of analyzing a cryptocurrency project is examining the team, the technology, and the community support. Strong and seasoned personnel, reliable and transparent technology, and an active and encouraging community can all help

ensure the project's success and long-term viability.
To ensure you are making well-informed investment
decisions, do extensive research, double-check facts,
and consult reliable sources.

CHAPTER 6: SECURELY STORING YOUR CRYTO ASSETS

The protection of your cryptocurrency holdings is crucial. A secure storage solution that guards your private keys against loss, theft, and hacking is essential if you want to preserve your digital capital. The following techniques can help you store your cryptocurrency assets safely:

1. Hard Copy wallets:

Hardware wallets are actual objects made for offline cryptocurrency private key storage. Since they're not online, they offer an additional degree of protection. Ledger Nano S, Ledger Nano X, and Trezor are a few well-known hardware wallets.

The advantages are as follows: superior security, defense against cyberattacks, and ease of usage.

Cons: Cost (there is an initial investment required), possible gadget loss risk.

2. Wallets made of paper:

Printing your public addresses and private keys on paper is the process of using a paper wallet. You must use great caution to prevent physical damage and theft to the paper while using this method to keep your keys offline.

 High degree of security and lack of electronic vulnerabilities are its pros.

Cons: Drawbacks: Not ideal for frequent transactions, susceptible to physical harm, and paper wallet loss.

3. Desktop and mobile software wallets:

Applications known as software wallets are those that you can install on your desktop computer or mobile device to store cryptocurrency. They can be hacked and infected with malware, despite their convenience. Trust Wallet (mobile) and Electrum (desktop) are two examples.

Pros: Easy to use, frequently free.

Cons: Hacking and malware vulnerability; some features require an internet connection.

4. Chilled Warehouse:

The term "cold storage" describes the process of keeping your private keys completely offline. This can involve keeping keys in a secure location in a non-digital format or even using hardware or paper wallets.

High security and defense against internet attacks are its advantages.

Cons: Less convenient for regular transactions; possible loss if not handled properly.

5. Wallets with several signatures:

To approve a transaction, multisignature wallets need several private keys. For instance, two of the three private keys in a 2-of-3 multisig wallet might be required to finish a transaction. This method provides an additional degree of security.

Pros: Better security and defense against single points of failure.

Cons: Requires several private key holders and is complex.

6. Safe Recovery and Backup:

Make secure backups of your recovery phrases or private keys at all times, regardless of the storage option you select. These backups should be kept in several safe places. Make sure that in the event of an emergency, reliable people are aware of how to access your cryptocurrency holdings.

7. Refrain from using exchange and online wallets:

Steer clear of holding sizable amounts of cryptocurrency on exchanges or in online wallets. Hacking and theft are more likely to occur with these wallets.

8. The usage of two-factor authentication (2FA):

For any wallets or accounts that support it, enable two-factor authentication (2FA). A second line of defense is added when gaining access to your assets using 2FA.

9. Update and secure your devices regularly:

Ensure that the devices you use to transact with cryptocurrencies are kept up to date, have secure passwords, and have security software installed.

10. Remain Educated:

Keep up with the most recent security procedures and risks in the Bitcoin world. Be wary of fraud and phishing efforts.

Keep in mind that maintaining security requires constant attention, so you need to be careful with the assets you have in cryptocurrencies. Depending on your unique requirements and usage habits, it's critical to find a balance between security and accessibility.

6:1 The Importance of Wallets

Wallets for cryptocurrencies are essential to the ecosystem since they operate as the entry point for organizing, safeguarding, and transferring digital assets. They are essential to the cryptocurrency industry for several reasons.

1. Security:

Wallets for cryptocurrencies offer a safe way to keep your private keys, which are necessary for controlling and accessing your digital assets. You lower your risk of theft, hacking, and unauthorized access to your money by storing your private keys in a wallet.

2. Mastery:

You have complete control over the cryptocurrency assets you own using wallets. Your assets can be sent, received, and managed independently of a bank or other financial organization. One of the fundamental tenets of cryptocurrencies is control, which emphasizes financial independence and self-sovereignty.

3. privacy:

Because cryptocurrency wallets let you create and manage several addresses for your transactions, they provide a certain level of secrecy. To a certain extent, this can assist in safeguarding your financial information and identity.

4. Obtainability:

Wallets can be found in a variety of formats, such as mobile, software, and hardware wallets.

Accessibility for users with various requirements and preferences is made possible by this diversity. You can select a wallet based on your technical proficiency and lifestyle.

5. Convenience:

Wallets for cryptocurrencies are quite portable. Anywhere there is an internet connection, you may access your money and conduct transactions. Travel and overseas remittances benefit greatly from this mobility.

6. Capital Outlay:

Wallets provide a safe place to keep and store cryptocurrency for investors with longer time horizons. For people who purchase and hold digital assets in the hopes of seeing their value increase over time, this is crucial.

7. Blending in:

Wallets for cryptocurrencies let you manage many digital assets at once. For people who own numerous tokens and cryptocurrencies, this is quite crucial. You can effectively track the success of your investments and diversify your holdings.

8. Decentralization:

You support the decentralized aspect of cryptocurrencies by utilizing wallets. Your financial management is not outsourced to a single organization. This is consistent with the fundamental ideas of cryptocurrency and blockchain technology.

9. Steer clear of exchange risks:

Entrusting your money to Bitcoin exchanges puts you at risk of hacking, bankruptcy, and changes in regulations. By giving you independent control over your assets through wallet use, you can lower the risks involved with holding exchange-traded securities.

10. International Trade:

Wallets for cryptocurrencies make it relatively simple to conduct cross-border transactions. International remittances are quicker and more affordable when you can transfer and receive digital assets directly from the sender and recipient without the use of middlemen.

wallets for cryptocurrencies are necessary equipment for everybody working in the field. They give consumers accessibility, security, control, and privacy while allowing them to manage their digital assets in a decentralized, self-governing way. Prioritizing security and selecting a wallet that suits your needs are essential when it comes to storing and handling cryptocurrency.

6:2 Hot Wallets vs. Cold Wallets

The two main types of Bitcoin wallets are hot wallets and cold wallets, both with pros and cons. It's essential to comprehend their distinctions to select the best wallet for your wants and priorities:

Hot Wallets:

Hot wallets are digital currency wallets that are always available for online transactions and are linked to the Internet. They are frequently utilized for regular digital asset trading and spending. Among the popular varieties of hot wallets are:

1. Virtual wallets: These are web-based wallets offered by online wallet providers or cryptocurrency exchanges. It can be viewed using a web browser.

2. Touchscreen Wallets: These are mobile-device-specific wallet apps. They are usually internet-connected and convenient for transactions while on the go.

3. Desktop Wallets: Software wallets that you can install on your PC. When your PC is connected to the internet, you can view them.

The advantages of hot wallets:

Friendliness: Hot wallets are convenient for regular transactions because they are simple to use and access.

Quick Transactions: They make cryptocurrency transfers quick and easy.

Friendly to Users: Many hot wallets are made with ease of use and accessibility in mind, making them ideal for novices.

The drawbacks of hot wallets

Dangers to Security: Because hot wallets are online, they are more susceptible to malware, phishing scams, and hacking.

Not Suitable for Extended Storage: For this reason, they are not recommended for long-term storage of significant quantities of cryptocurrency because of increased security threats.

Cold wallets:

Cold wallets are cryptocurrency wallets meant for long-term, safe storage of digital assets that are not linked to the internet. Usually, they are kept for savings or investment purposes when holding cryptocurrencies. Typical forms of cold wallets include:

1. hardware wallets: Physical devices that keep private keys offline. They offer excellent security and defense against internet dangers.

2. Notecard Wallets: Printing public addresses and private keys on actual paper is the process of creating a paper wallet. It completely removes the need for keys, although handling it carefully is necessary to avoid physical harm.

3. Cold Storage Devices: Dedicated cold storage devices provide better security for long-term storage by maintaining private keys offline.

The advantages of cold wallets:

Protection: Cold wallets are incredibly safe and guard against malware and other internet dangers like hacking.

Perfect for Extended Storage: They are appropriate for long-term storage of substantial sums of bitcoin.

Protection against Online Risks: Cold wallets shield your valuables against the dangers of online exchanges and wallets.

The drawbacks of cold wallets

Restricted Availability: Because cold wallets are offline, they are not appropriate for regular transactions.

Curve of Learning: There can be a learning curve with certain cold wallet features, especially for new users.

Price: Cold storage units and hardware wallets are not cheap upfront.

the decision between hot and cold wallets is based on your unique requirements. Hot wallets provide speed and ease of use for regular transactions, but there is a higher chance of security issues. Cold wallets put security first and work best for long-term storage, although they could be harder to access for regular transactions. Many Bitcoin users choose to utilize both in conjunction, storing their cryptocurrency in secure cold wallets and using hot wallets for daily transactions.

6:3 Protecting Your Private Keys

The most important part of Bitcoin security is private keys. They provide you access to your digital assets, and you run the danger of losing your cryptocurrency holdings if they end up in the wrong hands. The following are crucial actions to safeguard your private keys:

1.Employ hardware wallets:

Think about utilizing a hardware wallet, like a Trezor or Ledger. Your private keys are stored offline on these physical devices, shielded from online risks like malware and hackers. Among the safest ways to keep cryptocurrency is using a hardware wallet.

2. Produce Robust, Distinct Keys:

Make careful to produce your private keys using robust cryptographic algorithms when you create a wallet. Always utilize wallet software from reliable sources, and stay away from weak or keys.

3. Maintain Backups:

Make safe duplicates of your private keys. Make several copies and keep them in various secure places. For backup, think about utilizing paper wallets or encrypted USB devices.

4. Safe Digital Restores:

Make sure your digital backups are password- and encryption-protected if you decide to use them. For these files, create strong, one-of-a-kind passwords that you update frequently.

5. Guard Hard Copy Backups:

Keep any physical backups you may have, like paper wallets or hardware wallet recovery seeds, in a safe place that is protected from fire. Keep them safe from theft and physical harm.

6. Make Use of a Secure Setting:

Private keys should never be generated or entered in an unprotected or public setting. To manage your cryptocurrency, use a reputable, well-maintained computer or other device.

7. Steer clear of online key generation:

Steer clear of websites or online programs that produce private keys. These could be dangerous and jeopardize your keys' security.

8. Use Paper Wallets With Care:

Paper wallets can be safe, but they can also be lost, stolen, or physically damaged. If you carry a paper wallet, handle and store it with great caution.

9. Utilize multi-signature wallets:

If you want to authorize transactions with numerous private keys, think about utilizing multi-signature wallets. By doing this, you may increase security and safeguard against single points of failure.

10. Turn on 2FA or two-factor authentication:

Turn on two-factor authentication (2FA) if your exchange or wallet supports it. When gaining access to your accounts, 2FA provides an additional degree of security.

11. Don't Share Your Private Keys:

Your recovery phrases and private keys should never be shared with anybody. Hackers and scammers might try to fool you into disclosing this information.

12. Confirm the addresses:

Verify the recipient's address twice before sending cryptocurrency. Errors may result in permanent losses. Numerous wallets allow address verification by copy-and-paste or QR code scanning.

13. Watch Out for Phishing Schemes:

Watch out for phishing efforts through websites or emails. Before submitting your private keys or other sensitive information, always make sure the source is legitimate.

14. Update Software Frequently:

Update the operating system, security software, and wallet software. Bug fixes and security improvements are frequently included in updates.

15. Take Estate and Legal Planning Into Account:

Think about estate and legal planning for your cryptocurrency holdings in case of unanticipated events. Make sure your trusted people or heirs know how to obtain your private keys in case something happens to them.

16. Get Knowledge:

Keep up with the most recent security procedures and risks about cryptocurrencies. Update your knowledge often to adjust to evolving dangers.

You may greatly improve the security of your private keys and guard your Bitcoin holdings against loss and theft by following these procedures. When using cryptocurrency, security should always come first.

CHAPTER 7: BUYING AND SELLING CRYPTOCURRENCIES

Purchasing and trading cryptocurrencies requires several procedures, from picking a trustworthy exchange to safely maintaining your funds. Here is a manual to help you through the procedure:

Purchasing Digital Assets:

1. Select a Cryptocurrency Exchange: Choose a trustworthy cryptocurrency exchange to purchase and sell virtual assets. Bitstamp, Kraken, Binance, and Coinbase are a few of the well-known exchanges.

2. Create an Account: Open an account on the exchange of your choice. By Know Your Customer

(KYC) rules, you will be required to furnish personal information for identification verification.

3. Secure Your Account: To increase security, turn on two-factor authentication (2FA). Make sure your exchange account password is strong and distinct.

4. Deposit Funds: Funds your exchange account with fiat money (such as USD or EUR). Frequently, bank transfers, credit/debit cards, and other payment options accepted by the exchange can be used for this.

5. Select Your Digital Asset: After funding your account, choose the cryptocurrency you wish to purchase. Learn about the cryptocurrency's use cases and past price movements by doing some research.

6. Place an Order: Choose between a limit order, which specifies a price at which you want to buy,

and a market order, which buys at the going rate. Enter the desired amount to buy cryptocurrency.

7. Check and Verify: Verify again the specifics of your order, such as the quantity and cost. Verify the order, and it will be fulfilled in line with the order type you selected.

8. Secure Storage: You should think about moving your cryptocurrency to a secure wallet after purchasing. Options for safe storage include paper wallets, software wallets, and hardware wallets.

Cryptocurrency Sales:

1. Select an Exchange for Cryptocurrencies: Select the exchange where you wish to sell your digital assets if you aren't using the same one where you bought the bitcoin.

2. Create an Account: Open a new exchange account. You can use the same account that you used throughout the purchase procedure.

3. Secure Your Account: Just like when making a purchase, make sure your exchange account is protected by 2FA and has a strong, one-of-a-kind password.

4. Make a cryptocurrency deposit: Move the bitcoin from your wallet to the exchange that you wish to sell. Make sure the wallet address you're sending it to is correct.

5. Place an Order: Select if you wish to sell using a limit order or a market order. Enter the desired selling amount of cryptocurrency.

6. Check and Confirm: Check the order information, making sure the quantity and cost are correct. Verify

the order, and it will be fulfilled in line with the order type you selected.

7. Retrieve Money: You can withdraw the fiat money you received from the sale or another cryptocurrency after selling. Move it to a different wallet or your bank account.

8. Safe Deposit Box: If you plan to hold onto the money rather than take it right away, you might want to move it to a safe wallet.

Advice on Purchasing and Dealing in Cryptocurrencies:

- Do your homework: Learn everything you can about the potential and use cases of the cryptocurrency you're interested in before making a purchase.

- Start small: If you've never traded cryptocurrencies before, think about making a modest initial investment to get some experience.

- Stay informed: Stay up to current on market movements, regulatory changes, and cryptocurrency news that could affect your trading choices.

- Manage your risk by not investing more than you can bear to lose. The markets for cryptocurrencies can be unpredictable.

- Tax compliance: Keep correct records and be informed about your nation's tax requirements regarding cryptocurrency transactions.

- Steer clear of scammers: Keep an eye out for phishing scams, fraudulent schemes, and deals that appear too good to be true.

- Seek professional advice: You should think about speaking with financial and legal specialists if you have any questions concerning your tax responsibilities, investing plan, or any other facet of trading cryptocurrencies.

Trading cryptocurrencies have the potential to be profitable, but there are hazards involved. You can move through the process more securely and successfully if you pay attention to these instructions and proceed with caution.

7:1 Steps to Purchase Cryptocurrencies

Several procedures must be followed to buy cryptocurrency: choosing an exchange, opening an account, depositing money, and carrying out your purchase order. Here's a detailed how-to:

1. Select an Exchange for Cryptocurrencies:
- Find a trustworthy Bitcoin exchange by doing some research. Gemini, Bitstamp, Kraken, Coinbase, and Binance are a few well-liked choices. Make sure the cryptocurrency you wish to purchase is supported by the exchange.

2. Create an Account:
- Open an account on the exchange of your choice. You will be required to submit personal data and adhere to identity verification protocols, such as Know Your Customer (KYC) guidelines

3. Secure Your Account:

- To increase security, turn on two-factor authentication (2FA). Make sure your exchange account password is strong and distinct.

4. Deposit Funds:

- Funds your exchange account with fiat money (USD, EUR, or your local currency, for example). Bank transfers, credit/debit cards, and other payment methods provided by the exchange are typical ways to make deposits.

5. Select Your coin:

- After funding your account, choose the coin you wish to buy. Learn about the technology, use cases, and price history of the cryptocurrency by doing some research.

6. Place an Order:

- Select if you wish to place a limit or market order:

Market Order: buy the coin at the going rate in the market. This kind of order is carried out immediately .

Restricted Order: Indicate the price you wish to pay for the coin. When the market price equals the amount you have requested, the order is executed.

7. Input the Quantity:
 - Indicate how much cryptocurrency you wish to buy. Using the current exchange rate, the exchange will show an equal amount of fiat money.

8. Review and Confirm:
 - Verify the specifics of your order, such as the quantity and cost. Verify the order, and it will be fulfilled in line with the order type you selected.

9. Secure Storage:

- For extra security, think about moving your cryptocurrency to a secure wallet after purchase. Options for safe storage include paper wallets, software wallets, and hardware wallets.

10. Remain Up to Date:

 - Keep abreast of market developments and cryptocurrency news. Since market conditions are subject to sudden changes, being informed will help you make wise decisions.

11. Tax Considerations:

- Recognize your nation's tax requirements regarding bitcoin transactions. To ensure proper tax reporting, maintain thorough records of all of your transactions.

12. Practice Risk Management:

- Because cryptocurrency markets can be extremely unpredictable, don't invest more than you can afford to lose.

You will buy cryptocurrency safely and successfully by following these instructions and doing extensive research. To safeguard your investments, use a reliable exchange and implement security measures. To properly manage risk, you should also think about diversifying your portfolio and keeping an eye on the long term.

7:2 How to Trade on Cryptocurrency Exchanges

Buying and selling digital assets on cryptocurrency exchanges is the process of trading to capitalize on price movements. Here's a detailed tutorial on using an exchange to trade cryptocurrencies:

1. Select a Cryptocurrency Exchange:
 - Decide on a trustworthy exchange for cryptocurrencies. Binance, Coinbase Pro, Kraken, and Bitstamp are a few well-liked choices. Make sure the cryptocurrency you wish to trade is supported by the exchange.

2. Create an Account:
- Open an account on the exchange of your choice. It will usually be necessary for you to comply with Know Your Customer (KYC) rules by providing

personal information and completing identification
verification.

3. Secure Your Account:
 - To increase security, turn on two-factor
authentication (2FA). Make sure your exchange
account password is strong and distinct.

4. Deposit Funds:
- Funds your exchange account with fiat money
(USD, EUR, etc.) or other cryptocurrencies. Bank
transfers, credit/debit card purchases, and
cryptocurrency deposits are typical deposit methods.

5. Pick a Trade Pair:
 - Decide the trading pair you wish to engage in.
Two cryptocurrencies, such as BTC/USD,
ETH/BTC, or LTC/EUR, make up a trading pair.
You exchange one currency for another.

6. Select Your Order Type:

 - Choose the kind of order you wish to submit.

 Market Order: Purchase or dispose of at the going rate. Market orders are filled right away.

Restricted Order: Indicate the price you're willing to sell or acquire at. When the market price equals the amount you have requested, the order is executed.

7. Input the Quantity:

 - Type in the amount of cryptocurrency you wish to trade. The equal amount in the other currency of the trading pair will be shown by the exchange.

8. Review and Confirm:

 - Verify the quantity, price, and trading pair of your order by double-checking the details. Verify the command to carry it out. If you put in a limit order, it will be filled when the market hits the price you designated.

9. Watch the Market:
- Keep a watch on price changes and other pertinent information. Charts, news, and technical analysis are all useful tools for traders.

10. Set Stop-Loss and Take-Profit Orders (Optional):
- You can limit risk and automatically execute trades at particular price levels by setting stop-loss and take-profit orders on several exchanges.

11. Trading Strategies:
- Use a trading plan that is in line with your objectives. Common tactics include day trading, swing trading, and long-term holding.

12. Manage Risk:

- Use stop-loss orders and risk-reward ratios, and don't invest more than you can afford to lose to manage risk.

13. Be Informed:

 - Stay current on market developments and cryptocurrency news. Since market conditions are subject to sudden changes, being informed will help you make wise decisions.

14. Tax Considerations:

 - Recognize your nation's tax requirements for bitcoin trading. To file taxes, maintain precise records of your trades.

15. Withdraw Funds:

 - Transfer money to your wallet or bank account after you've made profitable trades or need to relocate assets to safekeeping.

16. Continuous Learning:

- Trading cryptocurrencies can be tricky and dangerous. Continue to learn and hone your trading techniques in light of your experiences and expertise.

It's critical to remember that there are hazards associated with trading cryptocurrencies and that markets can move wildly. Avert FOMO (fear of missing out) by making well-informed decisions and refraining from investing more than you can afford to lose. When it comes to trading, security and risk management should always come first.

7:3 Understanding Trading Orders

You can direct a cryptocurrency exchange to purchase or sell digital assets at a given price and under specific terms by giving them trading orders. You can execute trades in numerous ways with each order type, each of which has a distinct function. Some typical trading orders are as follows:

1.A market order :

-market orderis a request to buy or sell a cryptocurrency at the going rate on the market. It is carried out right away. Market orders are simple to use and guarantee a speedy completion of your trade. However, due to market volatility, the precise execution price could change.

2. Limit Order:

-With a limit order, you can choose the exact price at which you wish to purchase or dispose of a coin.

The order is only filled when the market hits the price you have set, or a higher one. Limit orders provide you greater control over the price at which they are executed, but they might not be filled if the market moves past your limit.

3. Stop Order (Take-Profit and Stop-Loss):
- Stop orders are employed to safeguard profits or restrict possible losses. These two kinds are:

Cease-Loss Request: This order is positioned above the market price for a purchase order and below the price at which a sell order is currently being placed. The order becomes a market order and is executed at the current market price when the market hits the stop price.

Order of Take-Profit: A take-profit order is positioned above the current market price for a sell order and below the current market price for a purchase order, much like a stop-loss order. When the market hits the designated price, it locks in profits.

4. Order of Trailing Stop:
 - A dynamic stop order that follows the price of the market is called a trailing stop order. If the market price moves in your favor, the trailing stop keeps the predetermined percentage or difference in price. The order is executed and turns into a market order if the price reverses by the designated amount.

5. Fill or Kill (FOK) Order:
- An order to fill or kill is intended to be carried out either completely or not at all. The exchange cancels the order if it is unable to complete the total amount right away. When you want to make sure that your order is filled completely and without any partial fills, you use FOK orders.

6. Instant or Cancel (IOC) Order:

- Except that it permits partial fills, an instant or cancel order is comparable to a fill or kill order. The exchange will execute the part that can be completed and cancel the remainder if it is unable to fulfill the entire order right away.

7. Good 'Til Canceled (GTC) Order:

- Until the trader executes or cancels the order, a GTC order is in effect. These orders have no set expiration date and are frequently utilized for longer-term strategies.

8. Day Order:

- Only the current trading day is covered by a day order. It is automatically canceled if it is not completed by the conclusion of the trading day.

9. Iceberg Order:

- With an iceberg order, you can place a sizable order while hiding the total amount. It is more difficult for others to ascertain the complete extent of your deal when only a piece of the order is visible in the order book.

It is essential to comprehend these order types to trade cryptocurrencies successfully. Depending on your trading strategy and objectives, each form of order offers advantages and applications of its own. Before you trade with real money, you should become familiar with the order options offered by your selected exchange and practice using them in a risk-free environment.

CHAPTER 8: STRATEGIES FOR PROFITABKE INVESTIN

While investing in cryptocurrencies has the potential to be very successful, there are hazards involved. To increase your chances of success and reduce your possible losses, think about these profitable cryptocurrency investing strategies:

1. Diversification:
- Invest in a range of digital assets to diversify your Bitcoin portfolio. Refrain from investing all of your money in a single cryptocurrency. Spreading out risk and maximizing profits from a variety of assets can be achieved through diversification.

2. HoDLing, or Long-Term Holding:
-Think about the long-term investing approach known as "HODLing." Purchasing cryptocurrencies

and holding them for a long time—often during market volatility—is the goal of this strategy. It seeks to capitalize on digital assets' potential for long-term growth.

3. Risk Management:
 - Never take on more debt by investing than you can comfortably lose. For your cryptocurrency investments, establish a clear budget and follow it. To reduce possible losses, use stop-loss orders and other risk management instruments.

4. Information Gathering and Vigilance:
-Do your homework on cryptocurrencies before investing. Recognize the technology, use case, group, and community that are behind a project. Be updated with news and market developments that could affect your investment decisions.

5. Fundamental Analysis:

- Use this method to evaluate a cryptocurrency's worth. Considerations include the team, technology, market need, and adoption of the project. Think about the real-world use of cryptocurrencies and the issue they seek to resolve.

6. Technical Analysis:
- Examine price charts using technical analysis to spot trends and patterns. Making well-informed decisions on entry and exit can be aided by technical analysis. Relative Strength Index (RSI), moving averages, and support/resistance levels are a few metrics you might want to use.

7. Dollar-Cost Averaging (DCA):
- Use a dollar-cost averaging technique by consistently making fixed cryptocurrency investments at predetermined intervals (e.g., weekly or monthly). DCA can be beneficial for long-term

holdings as it lessens the effect of market volatility on your investments.

8. Set Clear Goals:

 - Specify your time frame and investment objectives. Are you aiming for long-term financial objectives like retirement or are you just seeking quick money? Your goals will determine how you approach things.

9. Avoid Emotional Trading:

 - Poor trading results are frequently the result of emotional decision-making. Adhere to your pre-planned plan and refrain from making snap decisions about purchases or sales out of fear or greed.

10. Safe Storage:

- Invest in hardware wallets or other safe wallets to guard your valuables against loss and hacking. Safeguard your recovery phrases and private keys.

11. Continuous Learning:
- Keep up with developments in technology and the bitcoin market. The environment is constantly changing, and education is a continuous process.

12. Legal and Tax Compliance:
- Recognize and abide by your jurisdiction's cryptocurrency-related tax laws. For tax reporting purposes, keep thorough records of all of your transactions.

13. Remain Alert:
 - Be on the lookout for fraud, shady businesses, and ventures that guarantee profits. Sometimes, something is too good to be true.

14. Professional Advice:

- Take into account consulting financial professionals, particularly when it comes to intricate tax planning and estate matters.

Remember that the price of cryptocurrencies can fluctuate greatly and that the markets are quite speculative. Although they are feasible, profitable investments are never assured. If you want to increase your chances of making money in the cryptocurrency market, evaluate your risk tolerance, do extensive research, and make wise investments.

8:1 HODLing: The Long-Term Approach

A long-term investment tactic in the cryptocurrency space is called "HODLing." The term "HODL" was coined to refer to an investment strategy that has gained popularity among investors who see the long-term potential of digital assets, although it was first misspelled in a Bitcoin forum post. This is a summary of hoarding:

HODLing: What is it?

Buying cryptocurrencies and sticking onto them for a long time—often disregarding short-term market fluctuations—is known as hollering. The basic goal of hoarding cryptocurrency is to withstand the need to trade frequently and to hold onto a strong belief in the cryptocurrency's long-term value.

Fundamental Ideas of HODLing:

1. Compassion: HOLDers are patient investors who think that cryptocurrency values will rise in the future. They are prepared to put up with turbulence in the market without losing hope.

2. Minimize Emotional Trading: By sticking to their assets despite momentary price fluctuations, HOLDers want to lessen the impact of emotion on their decision-making. They don't buy or sell because they are greedy or afraid.

3. Long-Term Vision: Most HOLDers have an investment horizon that spans years or perhaps decades in the future. They don't give as much thought to transient price changes.

Properties of Holding:

1. Investing in Long-Term Development: The goal of HOLDers is to profit from cryptocurrency's potential for long-term growth. They think that the potential for digital assets to transform technology and finance will result in significant value growth.

2. Decreased Trading Expenses:
 HODLers avoid frequent trading and related expenses, such as transaction fees and capital gains taxes, by keeping assets for an extended period.

3. Fundamental Analysis is the Focus: Fundamental analysis is frequently given precedence over technical analysis by HOLDers. They concentrate on comprehending a cryptocurrency's technology, use case, team, and acceptance to evaluate its long-term potential.

4. Streamlined Approach: Because it doesn't call for frequent market monitoring or active trading, HODLing can be a simple investing approach.

HODLing's Risks and Challenges:

1. Volatility of the Market: Investors who hold cryptocurrency must put up with considerable price swings because the markets can be very unstable. It can be difficult for some investors to exercise patience in down markets.

2. Lack of Liquidity: Because HODLing can tie up resources for long periods, it is not as appropriate for people who require access to cash for urgent needs.

3. Value Loss Risk: Although there are potential long-term benefits for cryptocurrencies, there are no

assurances of financial gain. Over time, cryptocurrencies may potentially lose value.

4. Inflexibility: HODLers risk missing out on profitable possibilities if they don't take advantage of market swings or engage in shorter-term trading techniques.

Are You a Good Fit for HODLing?

Those who have the patience to keep assets through market ups and downs and a strong belief in the future of cryptocurrencies are good candidates for the HODLing method. Those who are risk cautious or in need of funds for urgent financial requirements could find it unsuitable.

Ultimately, your financial objectives, risk tolerance, and market forecast will determine whether you choose to hold onto your investments or use other tactics. Before choosing to take a HODLing method for bitcoin investing, you must carry out extensive research and take into account your unique situation.

8:2 Day Trading and Swing Trading

In the bitcoin market, day trading and swing trading are two common short- to medium-term trading techniques. While purchasing and selling digital assets is a part of both strategies, their approaches and timelines are different. This is a synopsis of both tactics:

Trading by Day:

Duration: Buying and selling cryptocurrencies inside the same trading day is known as day trading, and it is a short-term strategy. One place is hard for them to stay for a long time.

Notable Features:

1. Repeated Trading: Day traders do several trades to profit from brief price swings throughout the day.

2. Day-to-Day Evaluation: To make snap judgments, day traders rely on technical analysis, which includes order book data, indicators, and chart patterns.

3. Control of Risk: Take-profit and stop-loss orders are frequently used by them to safeguard profits and reduce possible losses.

4. Attribution: Leverage is a tool used by certain day traders to increase the size of their trading positions and hence the possible returns and hazards.

5. High Focus and Stress: Because day trading is a fast-paced approach, it demands a great deal of focus and can be emotionally taxing.

Trading on the swings:

Duration: Swing trading is keeping positions open for a few days to a few weeks to profit from changes in price throughout that period.

Notable Features:

1. Reduced Deals: Compared to day traders, swing traders make fewer trades in search of chances with larger potential profits.

2. Fundamental and Technical Analysis: They evaluate market movements and the underlying worth of cryptocurrencies by fusing technical and fundamental analysis.

3. Control of Risk: Compared to day traders, swing traders are more carefree and frequently place stop-loss and take-profit orders.

4. Larger Time frames: Swing traders can conduct a more thorough study and reduce stress by basing their decisions on daily, weekly, or even monthly price charts.

5. Balanced Lifestyle: Those who enjoy a balanced lifestyle and don't want to spend their days glued to screens may find swing trading more appropriate.

Thoughts on Both Approaches:

1. Mission Control: It is advisable for day and swing traders to utilize risk management techniques, such as placing stop-loss orders and figuring out how much risk they can tolerate.

2. Analytical Studies: Success with either approach requires in-depth study, a thorough comprehension of cryptocurrencies, and market analysis.

3. Emotional Control: Trading decisions can be influenced by emotions. Regardless of the approach they take, traders need to manage their greed and anxiety.

4. Practice and Education: Before investing real money in trading, novice traders should educate themselves and practice virtual accounts.

5. Guidelines: Understand the laws and tax ramifications that apply to trading cryptocurrencies in your area.

What is the Best Strategy for You?

The decision between swing and day trading is influenced by your expertise level, personality, available time, and risk tolerance. Swing trading gives greater flexibility and can be better suited for people with other responsibilities, but day trading necessitates considerable concentration and stress tolerance.

Keep in mind that trading cryptocurrencies include risks and that the markets are often volatile. Both approaches have the potential to be lucrative, but they also call for both commitment and in-depth knowledge of the industry. Selecting the strategy that fits your objectives and skills is crucial.

8:3 Managing Risk and Setting Stop-Loss Orders

An essential component of effective bitcoin trading is risk control. Stop-loss orders are one of the best instruments for risk management. Here's how to properly use stop-loss orders and control risk:

Strategies for Risk Management:

1. Establish Your Tolerance for Risk: Decide how much risk you are willing to take on a single trade or for your entire portfolio before you begin trading. This is an essential stage in risk management.

2. Diversify Your Portfolio: To lower risk, distribute your investments among several cryptocurrencies. Refrain from investing all of your money in one single asset.

3. Position Sizing: Determine the right size position to take based on the distance to your stop-loss level and your risk tolerance. Steer clear of betting more than a small portion of your entire portfolio on one trade.

4. Employ stop-loss directives: An order to sell cryptocurrencies at a predetermined price in order to reduce possible losses is known as a stop-loss order. It provides protection should the market move against your position.

How to Set Stop-Loss Orders:

1. Select a Level of Stop Loss: To prevent losses, decide how much you can afford to lose on a trade. You should base your stop-loss level on your risk management plan, support/resistance levels, or technical analysis.

2. Consider Volatility: Be mindful of the cryptocurrency you are trading's volatility. Wider stop-loss levels could be necessary for more volatile assets in order to prevent premature triggers.

3. Create a Trailing Stop: Trailing stop orders are available on some exchanges. As the price swings in your favor, a trailing stop modifies your stop-loss level. This can lessen losses and assist ensure revenues.

4. Apply Technical Analysis: Chart patterns and technical indicators can assist you in determining appropriate stop-loss levels. One such strategy is to set a stop-loss immediately below a significant level of support.

5. Steer clear of emotional adjustments: Adhere to your stop-loss order once you've placed one. Refrain

from adjusting it hastily in reaction to transient price changes.

Guides for Efficient Risk Reduction:

1. Plan Your Trades: Make sure you have a well-defined plan before you initiate a trade. This plan should contain your take-profit and stop-loss levels.

2. Steer clear of overleveraging: Leverage can increase earnings, but it can also increase losses. Be mindful of your risk tolerance when using leverage.

3. Control Your Emotions: Greed and fear can cause hasty decisions. Remain true to your trading strategy and refrain from emotionally modifying your stop-loss orders.

4. Continually Evaluate and Modify: Review your risk management plan on a regular basis and make

necessary adjustments if your risk tolerance or the state of the market shifts.

5. Exercise Self-Control: In order to handle risks effectively, discipline is necessary. Follow through on your plan of action and refrain from acting rashly.

6. Ongoing Education: Remain aware and educated on the state of the bitcoin industry. Long-term success requires you to grow as a trader and learn from your experiences.

Through the application of risk management techniques and the skillful use of stop-loss orders, you may safeguard your investment and lessen the possible impact of unfavorable market fluctuations. Though there are no absolute assurances of success when trading cryptocurrencies, keep in mind that there are dangers involved. However, with careful risk management, your trading results can be greatly enhanced.

CHAPTER 9: TAXES AND LEGAL COMPLIANCE

When it comes to trading and investing in cryptocurrencies, taxes and legal compliance are important factors to take into account. What you should know:

1. Tax Requirements:

- Transactions using cryptocurrencies might be taxable in several places. Buying, selling, trading, mining, and receiving cryptocurrencies are just a few of the many kinds of transactions that tax authorities view as taxable events.

It's common to pay capital gains tax when you swap or sell cryptocurrency. The holding time and the nation's tax regulations may have an impact on the tax rate.

You must maintain thorough records of every cryptocurrency transaction you make, including the dates, quantities, and the transaction's value in local currency at the time.

2. Income Reporting:

- You must record Bitcoin as taxable income if you receive it as payment for goods or services. For tax computations, the cryptocurrency's value as of the moment of receipt is usually utilized.

- There are particular rules in several countries on how income from cryptocurrencies must be reported. Make sure you are familiar with the regulations in your area.

3. Mining-Related Tax Obligations:

- The benefits you get from mining cryptocurrency might be regarded as income. You could occasionally have to pay self-employment taxes as well.

Maintaining documentation of your mining operations is crucial, as is keeping track of the coins you've extracted and when you acquired them.

4. Airdrop and Fork Tax:

- There might be tax repercussions for airdrops, which distribute bitcoin for free, and forks, which break a blockchain into two distinct chains. The tax rules of your nation may apply to these events.

- To find out how to handle airdrops and forks for tax purposes, speak with a tax expert.

5. Maintaining Records:

- Tax compliance requires you to keep thorough and accurate records of all of your cryptocurrency transactions. To keep track of all of your transactions, including trades, transfers, sales, and purchases, use spreadsheets or software.

6. Seeking Expert Guidance:

- Tax laws about cryptocurrencies can be complicated and differ between nations. Seeking advice from a tax specialist or accountant with experience in bitcoin taxation is advised.

7. Adherence to Regulation:

- Keep yourself updated on the laws and rules about cryptocurrencies in your area. Recognize any licensing or reporting requirements that traders and companies using cryptocurrencies may have.

8. Know Your Customer (KYC) and Anti-Money Laundering (AML) Regulations:

Numerous bitcoin exchanges and service providers must abide by KYC and AML laws. These laws are intended to stop illegal actions like fraud and money laundering.

Provide identification and supporting documentation when utilizing cryptocurrency services that abide by these rules.

9. International Law:

Regulations about cryptocurrencies might differ greatly between nations. While some nations have welcomed cryptocurrencies, others have placed severe limitations or outright banned them.

- If you transact cryptocurrencies internationally, be mindful of the regulations of the country where you are conducting business as well as in your own country.

10. Stay Up to Date on Regulatory Shifts:

- The cryptocurrency regulatory environment is always changing. Stay informed about any changes to rules and regulations that might have an impact on your cryptocurrency-related activity.

One of the most important components of ethical bitcoin trading and investment is adhering to tax laws. Penalties and legal repercussions may follow noncompliance with these regulations. To make sure you are in complete compliance with all applicable rules and regulations in your country, it is essential to get advice from legal and tax professionals.

9:1 Cryptocurrency Taxation

Countries have different tax laws governing cryptocurrencies, and these laws can be complicated. For taxation purposes, it is critical to comprehend how your nation views cryptocurrencies. The following are some typical characteristics of taxing cryptocurrencies:

1. Cryptocurrency Classification:

For taxation purposes, cryptocurrencies are usually categorized in one of the following ways:

- Residence: Cryptocurrencies are regarded as property in several nations. This implies that, like with the sale of stocks or real estate, capital gains tax is levied on cryptocurrency exchanges or sales.

Value: Certain nations categorize cryptocurrencies as money and impose income taxes on anyone who mines, trades, or accepts them as payment.

2. Tax on Capital Gains:

- Capital gains tax is often imposed if cryptocurrencies are regarded as property in your nation. The profit you make from trading or selling cryptocurrency will be subject to taxation. Depending on how long (short-term or long-term) your holding period is, the tax rate may change.

3. Tax on Income:

- Transactions involving cryptocurrencies, such as mining and receiving payments, may be taxable in some states. It might be necessary for you to declare and pay income tax on any cryptocurrency earnings.

4. Documentation Needed:

- Tax authorities frequently demand you to declare cryptocurrency transactions. The date of the transaction, the quantity of cryptocurrency involved, and the corresponding value in your local currency at the moment of the transaction should all be included in these reports.

5. Maintaining Records:

- Tax compliance depends on keeping correct records of your cryptocurrency transactions. All transactions, including buys, sells, exchanges, and transfers, should be documented. Your tax due will be calculated using this information.

6. Tax Reductions:

- In certain circumstances, you might be able to write off costs associated with your cryptocurrency-related activities, like transaction fees or mining equipment. Consult your tax authority to find out what deductions are allowed.

7. Donations and Gifts of Cryptocurrency:

- The tax ramifications of cryptocurrency gifts and donations can vary. Contributions to charities may qualify for tax deductions, although gifts under a specific threshold may not be taxed in some countries.

8. Staking and Rewards for Cryptocurrencies:

- Rewards from staking and other Bitcoin activities are usually taxed as income. On these prizes, you might have to file taxes and make reports.

9. Forks and Airdrops:

- Tax ramifications may arise from airdrops and forks. You could have to record and pay taxes on the value you acquired from these events, depending on the tax regulations in your nation.

10. Speak with a Tax Expert:

- Since bitcoin taxation can be complicated, it's best to consult a tax specialist or accountant who specializes in cryptocurrency tax issues. They can guarantee that you abide by the law and assist you in understanding your tax responsibilities.

11. Tools for Tax Reporting:

- Tools for figuring out your tax liability and producing tax reports are available from certain cryptocurrency exchanges and tax software. These can help to streamline the reporting procedure.

Recall that tax laws are subject to change and that different nations and areas may have different policies regarding cryptocurrencies. Accurate tax compliance requires keeping up with the most recent tax developments and speaking with a tax expert. There may be fines and legal repercussions if cryptocurrency transactions are not reported or if cryptocurrency income is not taxed.

9: 2 Regulatory Challenges and Compliance

Governments and regulatory agencies around the world are having difficulty deciding how to approach and control this quickly developing technology, which presents several regulatory issues for the Bitcoin business. The following are some of the main legal obstacles and the steps needed to comply in the cryptocurrency space:

1. Absence of Standardized Regulations:

- There are issues since there isn't a unified regulatory framework for cryptocurrencies. Diverse national policies regarding the regulation or outright prohibition of cryptocurrencies have left investors and businesses in the dark.

2. Rules Regarding AML and KYC:

Cryptocurrency exchanges and service providers are required by Anti-Money Laundering (AML) and Know Your Customer (KYC) requirements to authenticate the identities of their users. Although observing these rules is vital to stopping illegal activity, people who are worried about their privacy may find it burdensome.

3. Adherence to Taxes:

- Tax authorities are paying more attention to transactions involving cryptocurrencies. It can be difficult and time-consuming to ensure tax requirements are followed, especially when it comes to declaring bitcoin holdings and transactions.

4. Regulation of Securities:

It can be difficult to decide if a certain cryptocurrency or initial coin offering (ICO) qualifies as a security. Cryptocurrency issuance and trading are impacted by onerous securities rules.

5. International Trade:

- Because cryptocurrencies allow for borderless transactions, it is difficult to implement legislation in different jurisdictions. Regulators are having difficulty controlling transactions that transcend borders.

6. Regulation and Decentralization:

- Regulators face difficulties because many cryptocurrencies are decentralized. Decentralized initiatives and blockchain networks might not be subject to traditional regulatory frameworks.

7. Safety of Customers:

Regulators' top goal is to shield consumers against fraud, con artists, and hazardous cryptocurrency investments. To protect the public, oversight and enforcement are crucial.

8. Regulation of STOs and ICOs:

- There has been heightened regulatory scrutiny of security token offerings (STOs) and initial coin offerings (ICOs). Transparency, investor protection, and adherence to securities regulations are crucial factors.

9. Central bank digital currencies (CBDCs) and stablecoins:

- The emergence of CBDCs and stablecoins begs the question of how the financial system will handle their regulation and integration.

10. Security and Privacy of Data:

- Cryptocurrency companies frequently deal with private user information. It is essential to abide by data privacy laws, such as the General Data Protection Regulation (GDPR).

11. Obstacles and Regulatory Gaps:

- Because the cryptocurrency market is so dynamic, legal frameworks may not keep up with advances in technology. New problems, such as non-fungible tokens (NFTs) and decentralized finance (DeFi), require regulators to adjust.

12. Surveillance Actions:

- Adherence to national and international legislation ought to be the top priority for cryptocurrency enterprises and individuals. AML and KYC processes, declaring Bitcoin profits for tax purposes, and abiding by securities regulations are a few examples of compliance methods.

- Contributing to rules and encouraging ethical behavior through interactions with government agencies and regulators can help mold the regulatory landscape.

-Maintaining current knowledge of the changing regulatory environment requires both ongoing education and legal counsel.

- Transparency can show a commitment to compliance, as can frequent reporting and clear terms and conditions for users.

- Software and solutions for regulatory technology (RegTech) can help companies manage regulatory compliance effectively.

- Law enforcement and regulators can trace unlawful activities on public blockchains with the use of blockchain analysis tools.

-Participating in self-regulatory activities and working with colleagues in the sector can help define best practices in the bitcoin area.

All things considered, the cryptocurrency sector needs to find a balance between encouraging innovation and safeguarding investors and customers. Building trust in the Bitcoin ecosystem and maintaining its long-term viability depends heavily on regulatory compliance.

9:3 Navigating Legal Frameworks

Because of the constantly changing nature of rules and the widespread use of cryptocurrencies, navigating the legal frameworks in the cryptocurrency business can be challenging. The following factors should be taken into account while addressing legal frameworks in the cryptocurrency space:

1. Recognize Your Authority:

Regulations about cryptocurrencies differ greatly between nations and regions. Understanding the particular legal requirements and rules in your jurisdiction is the first step. This covers laws about taxes, securities, and AML/KYC.

2. Classification of Regulations:

- Find out what category cryptocurrencies fall under in your jurisdiction. Are they regarded as assets, money, securities, or something else entirely? Regulation compliance and tax treatment are impacted by the classification.

3. Adherence to AML/KYC Guidelines:

- Know Your Customer (KYC) and Anti-Money Laundering (AML) laws are essential for Bitcoin exchanges and service providers. Make sure you abide by these rules by confirming user identification and reporting any questionable transactions.

4. Securities legislation:

- Be mindful of securities laws if you participate in Initial Coin Offerings (ICOs), Security Token

Offerings (STOs), or any other cryptocurrency that might be regarded as a security. Adherence to these laws is essential to prevent legal problems.

5. Adherence to Taxes:

- Recognize how Bitcoin transactions may affect your jurisdiction's taxes. Accurate reporting of Bitcoin income, profits, and losses is part of this.

6. Rules Regarding Data Privacy:

- Make sure your cryptocurrency company complies with data privacy laws, such as the General Data Protection Regulation (GDPR) in the European Union, if it manages user data.

7. Safety of Customers:

Put customer protection first by offering unambiguous terms and conditions, open disclosures, and dispute resolution procedures.

8. International Trade:

Cross-border transactions are made possible by cryptocurrencies. Recognize the ramifications of conducting business globally and make sure you adhere to all applicable government regulations.

9. Communicate with Authorities:

- You can better comprehend the regulatory environment and aid in the creation of responsible regulations by interacting with regulators and governmental organizations. Engage in dialogue and open consultations.

10. Consult a Lawyer:

Seeking advice from legal professionals with expertise in Bitcoin and blockchain laws is priceless. Legal counsel can guarantee local law compliance and offer advice on managing challenging legal matters.

11. Software and Tools for Compliance:

- Software and solutions for regulatory technology (RegTech) can assist in automating compliance procedures including transaction monitoring and AML/KYC checks.

12. Self-regulation by Industry:

- Take into account taking part in industry self-regulation programs that define best practices for the Bitcoin business. Both users and regulators may become more trusting as a result of these efforts.

13. Continuous Learning:

- Remain aware of how the law is changing about the Bitcoin sector. Since regulations can change quickly, ongoing education is crucial.

14. Openness:

- You may gain the trust of users, investors, and regulators by being transparent in your operations and financial reporting. Make it clear that you are committed to appropriate business practices and that you are working toward compliance.

15. Legal Hazards and Conflict Settlement:

- Be ready for potential legal issues and conflicts in the bitcoin space. Put procedures in place for resolving disputes and, if needed, taking legal action.

The legal frameworks are always changing, and the Bitcoin business is always developing. You can negotiate the legal system and create a reliable and compliant cryptocurrency firm by remaining informed, obtaining legal counsel, and interacting with regulators on a proactive basis.

CHAPTER 10: KEEPING UP WITH THE CRYTOPCURRENCY MARKET

For traders, investors, and fans, being up to date on the state of the cryptocurrency market is crucial. The world of cryptocurrencies is dynamic and always changing, so here are some tips to help you stay abreast of the most recent advancements:

1. Websites for Crypto News:

- Visit reliable blogs and websites with cryptocurrency news regularly. The most recent news, analysis, and insights can be found on websites like CoinDesk, CoinTelegraph, and CryptoSlate.

2. Forums for Cryptocurrencies:

- Participate in online groups and forums for cryptocurrencies, such as BitcoinTalk, Reddit's r/CryptoCurrency, and other sites where people talk about projects, news, and market trends.

3. Online Community:

- Keep up with Bitcoin projects, experts, and influencers on social media sites like YouTube, LinkedIn, and Twitter. When it comes to industry leaders' real-time updates, Twitter is particularly well-liked.

4. Apps for Cryptocurrency News:

On your smartphone, download Bitcoin news applications to get updates and push notifications while you're on the go.

5. Circulars and Billings:

- To have curated news delivered straight to your inbox, sign up for newsletters and email updates from influencers, market analysis platforms, and cryptocurrency websites.

6. Podcasts on Cryptocurrencies:

- Take a listen to podcasts on cryptocurrencies that discuss expert analysis, project updates, and market trends. A couple of well-known podcasts are "Unchained" and "The Pomp Podcast."

7. YouTube Channels for Cryptocurrencies:

- Watch YouTube channels devoted to blockchain technology and cryptocurrencies. A lot of content producers provide project evaluations, market research, and instructional materials.

8. Tools for Market Analysis:

- Use TradingView and CoinMarketCap, two platforms and tools for cryptocurrency market analysis, to get real-time market data, charts, and technical analysis.

9. Project websites and whitepapers:

- Read the whitepapers of cryptocurrency initiatives for in-depth information. For the most recent announcements and updates, check out the official websites of the projects that pique your interest.

10. Crypto Conferences and Events:

- Participate in virtual events, webinars, and conferences focused on cryptocurrencies to network with professionals in the field and gain knowledge of current advancements and trends.

11. Textbooks and Learning Materials:

- To increase your knowledge of cryptocurrency and blockchain technology, buy books and educational materials.

12. Revised Regulations:

- Monitor changes in regulations both locally and internationally. Recognize the potential effects of shifting regulations on the bitcoin market.

13. Reports on Market Analysis:

- Get market analyses and research reports from reliable sources. These papers frequently offer perceptions on potential investments and market trends.

14. Remain Alert to Security:

- Watch out for fraudulent schemes and phishing scams. For updates on cryptocurrencies, always double-check facts and consult reliable sources.

15. Sign up for Discord and Telegram Channels:

- A lot of Bitcoin communities and projects post news and updates on their Telegram and Discord channels. Sign up for pertinent channels to be updated.

16. Adhere to market indicators:

- Keep an eye on market indices for cryptocurrencies, such as the Crypto Fear & Greed Index, which might reveal emotion in the market.

17. Become Knowledgeable:

- Keep learning about market trends, cryptocurrency ventures, and blockchain technology. Making educated decisions requires having a solid understanding of the technology.

Recall that there can be tremendous volatility in the bitcoin market due to its high degree of speculation. Be cautious and do your research (DYOR). Keep yourself informed, but also approach the market with a long-term outlook and a well-thought-out risk management plan.

10: 1 The Role of News and Social Media

In the world of cryptocurrencies, news, and social media are crucial for forming opinions, affecting market patterns, and spreading knowledge. How they affect the bitcoin market is as follows:

1. State of the Market:

- Social media posts, tweets, and news stories can affect the mood of the market. Bullish sentiment is frequently sparked by positive news, whereas bearish sentiment can be sparked by negative news. Market prices are affected by the reactions of traders and investors to these feelings.

2. Volatility of Price:

Breaking news has the potential to significantly alter prices. Rapid price movements, for instance, may result from regulatory announcements, exchange hacking, or significant technology advancements.

3. Information Exchange:

- There is a constant flow of information on cryptocurrency projects, market trends, and new developments from news sources and social media platforms. To make wise selections, traders and investors need to have access to this information.

4. Sales of tokens and initial coin offerings (ICOs):

To attract investors, initial coin offerings (ICOs) and token sales frequently depend on news coverage and social media exposure. During these occasions, positive news may result in higher token prices.

5. Informing the Public:

- The mainstream adoption of cryptocurrencies and blockchain technology is facilitated by news and social media platforms that help spread awareness of these technologies.

6. Updates on Projects:

- News releases and social media are used by cryptocurrency projects to inform their communities about collaborations, technological developments, and project milestones.

7. Valuation Report:

-Experts and analysts frequently use news stories and social media to communicate their views, price forecasts, and market analyses. Trading decisions may be influenced by these studies.

8. Effect on Regulation:

- News about laws and policies from the government can have a big effect on the bitcoin market. Market turbulence and shifts in investor behavior may be brought about by regulatory changes.

9. Lies and Deceptions:

- News organizations frequently cover fraud and cryptocurrency scams. Those who read this material may be able to steer clear of such scams.

10. FUD and FOMO:

- Terms like Fear, Uncertainty, and Doubt (FUD) and Fear of Missing Out (FOMO) are frequently linked to bitcoin trading. When favorable developments are hyped in the media and news, they can create FOMO or FUD by disseminating false narratives.

11. Manipulating the Market:

- Market manipulation occasionally occurs through the use of social media platforms. Social media can be used to disseminate pump-and-dump schemes, in which the price of a cryptocurrency is artificially boosted by false information.

12. Information Exchange and Education:

- Social media and news are excellent resources for informing the public about blockchain technology, cryptocurrencies, and possible uses.

13. Establishing Community:

- Social media is essential to the development of communities around Bitcoin projects. On social media sites like Reddit, Discord, and Telegram, communities are frequently created where supporters and project teams communicate.

14. Instantaneous Updates:

- Real-time information on market prices, trading volumes, and other pertinent data are provided by cryptocurrency news websites and social media channels, which aid in keeping traders informed.

15. Worldwide Reach:

- News stories and social media have a global audience, enabling information to travel fast and affect markets in several time zones.

Although social media and news are excellent information sources, cryptocurrency traders, investors, and enthusiasts should proceed with care and due diligence (DYOR). Emotional responses can have a significant impact on market sentiment, and not all information is impartial or reliable. Identifying credible sources from hype is essential for making well-informed choices in the Bitcoin space.

10: 2 Reliable Information Sources

Making informed judgments in the Bitcoin space requires having access to accurate and trustworthy information. Here are a few reliable resources to keep up with news and developments about cryptocurrencies:

1. Trustworthy News Sources:

- Reputable and current sources of cryptocurrency news and analysis include CoinDesk, CoinTelegraph, CryptoSlate, and NewsBTC.

2. Exchanges for Cryptocurrencies:

- A lot of cryptocurrency exchanges have news sections and learning centers on their websites.

These may be excellent resources for learning about recent developments and market trends.

3. Official Websites for Projects:

- The official project website and whitepaper are the best places to find out more about particular cryptocurrencies. They frequently offer thorough details regarding the technology, team, and objectives of the project.

4. Subreddits and Forums for Cryptocurrencies:

- Community-driven news, talk, and information can be found on forums like BitcoinTalk and Reddit's r/CryptoCurrency. But, since information might originate from a variety of sources, always double-check it.

5. Reputable Twitter Users:

- Follow reliable analysts, project teams, and cryptocurrency professionals on Twitter. Several specialists use Twitter to deliver insightful information, news, and analysis.

6. Learning Environments:

- Websites such as Coinbase, Binance Academy, and Kraken's Crypto 101 offer instructional materials to assist with your understanding of the fundamentals of cryptocurrencies.

7. Podcasts on Cryptocurrencies:

Podcasts such as "Unchained," "The Pomp Podcast," and "What Bitcoin Did" showcase conversations and interviews with influential and knowledgeable people in the Bitcoin space.

8. Websites for Regulations:

- For updates on cryptocurrency laws and regulations, visit the websites of the financial and regulatory agencies in your area.

9. Tools for Market Analysis:

- Real-time data, charts, and tools for market analysis are available on websites like TradingView and CoinMarketCap.

10. Electronic Bulletins:

- To receive carefully selected news and updates straight to your inbox, sign up for email newsletters from respectable Bitcoin news sources and analysts.

11. Discord and Telegram Channels:

- For conversations and real-time updates, a lot of Bitcoin projects and communities keep up with Telegram and Discord channels. Follow the official channels to get up-to-date information.

12. Research papers and whitepapers:

Read research papers and whitepapers about a certain cryptocurrency to gain a better understanding of its objectives and technology. On the project's official website, these documents are frequently accessible.

13. Textbooks and Learning Materials:

- Comprehensive instructional resources may be found in books like "Crypto" by Eric Tyson and Kiana Danial and "Mastering Bitcoin" by Andreas M. Antonopoulos.

14. Academic Establishments:

- A few colleges and universities provide research and courses on blockchain and cryptocurrency technology. To gain in-depth information, think about enrolling in such programs.

15. Updates on Regulations:

- Follow statements from financial agencies and government press releases to stay up to date on regulatory changes.

16. Reputable YouTube Channels:

- Check out respectable YouTube channels that offer project reviews, market research, and instructional videos. Among the well-liked channels are "Crypto Daily" and "DataDash."

17. Data Providers and Market Indices:

- Keep an eye on market statistics and trends by following cryptocurrency market indexes such as the Crypto Fear & Greed Index and data sources like CoinGecko and CoinMarketCap.

Always double-check the facts you find from these sources, and take into account other viewpoints. Due diligence and critical thinking are crucial because the Bitcoin field is renowned for moving quickly and having the possibility of false information. Furthermore, exercise caution when relying on sources that might have a stake in endorsing particular initiatives or coins.

10:3 Tracking Market Trends and Sentiment

In the bitcoin market, it's critical to effectively monitor sentiment and market developments. Here are some tips and resources to keep you informed:

1.Technical analysis and price charts:

- Use charting software such as TradingView and CoinMarketCap to examine price changes, technical indicators, and support and resistance levels. You can find trends and possible entry and exit points with the use of technical analysis.

2. Websites with Market Data:

- To obtain real-time information on cryptocurrency prices, trading volumes, market capitalization, and historical data, visit websites that provide market data for cryptocurrencies, such as CoinGecko, CoinMarketCap, and CryptoCompare.

3. Tools for Sentiment Analysis:

- Sentiment and The TIE are two platforms that monitor social media, news, and forums for conversations on particular cryptocurrencies to give sentiment research.

4. News Compilers:

- Keep up with news aggregators for cryptocurrencies that gather press announcements, blog entries, and news stories. Keep abreast of the most recent advancements and how they might affect the market.

5. Reports on Cryptocurrency Analysis:

- Examine research studies provided by research firms and cryptocurrency analysts. These papers frequently offer in-depth analyses of project assessments, investment suggestions, and market trends.

6. Monitoring Social Media:

- Keep an eye out for cryptocurrency-related conversations on social media sites like Reddit, Twitter, and Telegram. Twitter is particularly well-liked for debates and real-time information.

7. Forums for Cryptocurrencies:

Engage in discussions and forums around cryptocurrencies, such as Reddit's r/CryptoCurrency and BitcoinTalk. Talking with others might yield insightful information and mood indicators.

8. Discord and Telegram Channels:

- Join the official Discord and Telegram channels for any cryptocurrency initiatives that pique your interest. Announcements, conversations, and updates are frequently posted on these channels.

9. Market Indices:

- Pay attention to market indexes for cryptocurrencies, such as the Crypto Fear & Greed Index and others, which gauge sentiment in the market and reveal the feelings of investors.

10. Indices of Sentiment:

- Sentiment indicators assist you in determining when the market is excessively bullish or bearish by offering insights into market sentiment. One

example of such an indicator is the Crypto Fear &
Greed Index.

11. Opinion pieces and blogs:

- Peruse the blogs and opinion pieces of reputable
analysts and specialists in the field of
cryptocurrency. These articles frequently offer
distinctive viewpoints on industry trends.

12. YouTube Channels and Podcasts:

- Take a listen to podcasts about cryptocurrencies
and subscribe to YouTube channels that offer news,
analysis, and professional viewpoints.

13. Lists on Twitter:

- Make Twitter lists to track and arrange influencers,
analysts, and specialists in cryptocurrencies. This

makes it easier for you to concentrate on pertinent information.

14. Email newsletters:

- To get handpicked news and insights delivered straight to your inbox, sign up for email newsletters from Bitcoin news sources and analysts.

15. Be Up to Date on Events:

- Pay attention to forthcoming cryptocurrency events, such as product launches, halvings, hard forks, and significant alliances. Trends and market sentiment may be impacted by these events.

16. Announcements from Regulators:

- Keep an eye on any regulatory announcements made by financial regulators and government bodies. Regulation modifications may have a big effect on market mood.

17. ICOs and Sales of Tokens:

- Keep abreast of impending token sales and initial coin offerings (ICOs), as these events have the potential to impact sentiment and market patterns.

To gain a comprehensive picture of market trends and mood, it is imperative to integrate many sources and indicators. Furthermore, keep in mind that the Bitcoin market is extremely volatile and speculative. Be cautious and incorporate the data you collect into a thorough trading or investing plan.

CHAPTER 11: CRYPTOCURRENCY AND THE FUTURE

Cryptocurrency has a bright future ahead of it and will probably have a big impact on a lot of different areas of technology, society, and money. The following are some important patterns and future directions to think about:

1. Adoption by Mainstream:

- Cryptocurrency is progressively integrating into the traditional banking system. Traditional financial institutions are incorporating digital assets into their offerings, and an increasing number of companies and individuals are accepting cryptocurrency payments.

2. Central Bank Digital Currencies:

- Several central banks are investigating the creation of CBDCs, or digital currencies issued by central banks. It is anticipated that these virtual versions of fiat money will coexist with cryptocurrencies and could provide new financial innovations and payment methods.

3. Defi (Decentralized Finance):

DeFi platforms, which provide decentralized lending, borrowing, trading, and yield farming, are transforming conventional financial services. DeFi can lessen the need for middlemen by offering financial services to neglected communities.

4. Intangible Assets (INTs):

- Because NFTs may be used to indicate ownership of distinct digital or physical things, they have become more and more popular. They are being used in gaming, art, collectibles, and other fields, opening up new possibilities for producers and consumers.

5. Smart Contracts :

- Smart contracts are automating and self-executing contracts thanks to blockchain technology. They are used in many different sectors, including supply chain management, real estate, and insurance.

6. Security and Privacy

- Concerns over data security and anonymity in the digital age are being addressed by the advent of privacy-focused cryptocurrencies and blockchain technologies.

7. Solutions for Scalability:

- Scaling methods, such as sharding (e.g., Ethereum 2.0) and Layer 2 solutions (e.g., Lightning Network for Bitcoin), attempt to solve blockchain scalability difficulties, increasing the effectiveness and affordability of cryptocurrencies.

8. Rules and Adherence:

- Laws enacted by governments to combat issues of fraud, money laundering, and investment protection are becoming more prevalent. Businesses and users of cryptocurrencies may feel more secure in the presence of clear regulatory frameworks.

9. Transfers Across Borders:

- By lowering costs and settlement times, cryptocurrencies have the potential to streamline cross-border transactions. This might significantly affect international trade and remittances.

10. Inclusion of Finances:

- People who lack or have limited access to banking services may be able to access the global economy through cryptocurrencies.

11. Progress in Technology:

The underlying blockchain technology is still developing, with new use cases, consensus techniques, and compatibility improvements.

12. Environmental Aspects to Consider:

- There is rising concern about how mining cryptocurrencies, particularly Proof of Work (PoW) blockchains, could affect the environment. There are efforts underway to find ways to mine more energy efficiently.

13. Knowledge and Sensitization:

- Users and investors need to be more informed about the advantages and disadvantages of cryptocurrencies as the market develops.

14. Market Maturity:

- A wider range of financial goods and services, enhanced infrastructure, and increased institutional involvement are signs that the bitcoin sector is maturing.

15. Difficulties and Unpredictability:

- Issues including market volatility, security threats, and regulatory changes remain. The world of cryptocurrencies is still unpredictable and dynamic.

The way cryptocurrencies develop, overcome obstacles, and work with current financial systems will determine their destiny. People and companies must be knowledgeable and use caution when navigating this quickly evolving environment. Although there are significant potential benefits, there are also risks, so success and long-term sustainability require careful planning.

11:1 The Evolution of Cryptocurrencies

Cryptocurrencies have advanced incredibly Since the launch of Bitcoin in 2009 . Here is a quick synopsis of their development:

1. Genesis of Bitcoin (2009):

- By using blockchain technology to build Bitcoin, the anonymous Satoshi Nakamoto popularized the idea of decentralized digital money. Its goal was to give users access to a peer-to-peer electronic cash system so they could conduct transactions without middlemen.

2. Altcoins and Litecoin (2011):

- The rise of competing cryptocurrencies, or "altcoins," was made possible by the popularity of Bitcoin. Litecoin, which denotes "silver" in contrast to Bitcoin's "gold," was among the initial cryptocurrencies to be released in 2011. Better technology was brought about by it, such as quicker block generation.

3. Proof of Stake (2012) Introduction:
 - Launched in 2012, Peercoin presented Proof of Stake (PoS) consensus as an alternative to Proof of Work (PoW) in Bitcoin. PoS sought to address issues with decentralization and energy efficiency.

4. Smart Contracts and Ethereum (2015):
 - Smart contracts were first proposed by Vitalik Buterin's Ethereum, which was launched in 2015. It extended the use cases beyond straightforward transactions by enabling developers to build programmable contracts and decentralized apps (DApps) on the blockchain.

5. Initial Coin Offerings (ICOs) (2017):

- The ICO craze of 2017 saw businesses raise money by launching their tokens on the Ethereum network. Legitimate projects as well as scams were drawn to the trend, which raised regulatory concerns.

6. The Boom in the Cryptocurrency Market (2017–2018):
 - With speculative trading and substantial growth, the cryptocurrency market saw an all-time high for Bitcoin. It also prompted the creation of a large number of fresh tokens and cryptocurrencies.

7. Cryptocurrency laws (Ongoing):
- To address concerns about fraud, money laundering, and investment protection, governments and regulatory agencies around the world started establishing frameworks and laws for cryptocurrencies.

8. Decentralized Finance (DeFi) (2020s):

-DeFi platforms, based on blockchain technology, offer decentralized financial services like trading, borrowing, and lending. DeFi's potential to upend conventional finance has drawn a lot of attention.

9. Non-fungible tokens (NFTs) (2021):

-NFTs are distinct digital assets that are represented on the blockchain. They gained popularity in 2021. They are employed in digital art, gaming, collectibles, and other artistic endeavors.

10. Digital Currencies Issued by Central Banks (CBDCs) (Continuous):

- Digital tokens of fiat currencies called CBDCs are being studied and tested by several central banks. The goal of these CBDCs is to offer inclusive and more effective payment methods.

11. Layer 2 Solutions and Scalability (Ongoing):

- To enhance scalability, lower transaction costs, and
boost transaction throughput, solutions such as the
Ethereum 2.0 and Bitcoin Lightning Network are
being developed.

12. Integration of Cryptocurrencies into Finance
(Ongoing):
- Conventional financial establishments, such as
investment firms, banks, and payment processors,
are incorporating cryptocurrencies into their
offerings.

13. Technological Advancements (Ongoing):
- Consensus methods, security, privacy, and
interoperability are just a few of the ways that
blockchain technology is getting better.

Although cryptocurrencies have grown and
innovated remarkably, they have also encountered
difficulties like market volatility, regulatory

changes, and security issues. The capacity of cryptocurrencies to overcome these obstacles, work with established financial institutions, and keep developing to satisfy the shifting demands of consumers and companies will determine how far they can go.

11:2 Real-World Applications and Adoption

Cryptocurrencies are slowly gaining traction across several industries and have a wide range of real-world uses. Here are a few major applications for cryptocurrencies:

1. Online Transfers:
 - Online payments using cryptocurrencies like Bitcoin and Ethereum are becoming more and more common. They provide a quick and safe means to conduct business, particularly for e-commerce and cross-border payments.

2. Remittances:
 - As an affordable substitute for conventional money transfer services, cryptocurrencies are being used to enable international remittances.

3. Virtual goods and gaming:

- In-game purchases, virtual assets, and blockchain-based games are just a few of the ways that the gaming industry uses cryptocurrencies and blockchain technology. A unique in-game item is represented by a non-fungible token (NFT).

4. Decentralized Finance (DeFi):
- Platforms for DeFi offer decentralized borrowing, trading, yield farming, and lending. Financial services are available to users without depending on conventional institutions.

5. Non-Fungible Tokens (NFTs):
- NFTs serve as ownership tokens for exclusive digital or tangible goods, such as virtual real estate, collectibles, music, and artwork. NFTs are exchanged, purchased, and sold over blockchain networks.

6. Supply Chain Management:

- Supply chains can be made more transparent and traceable by utilizing blockchain technology. It guarantees product authenticity and aids with the prevention of fraud.

7. Identity Verification:
- Users can safely share personal information and manage their digital identities with blockchain-based identity verification systems.

8. Tokenization of Assets:
- On blockchain systems, traditional assets like stocks, real estate, and commodities are tokenized to facilitate fractional ownership and simpler transfer.

9. Central Bank Digital Currencies (CBDCs)
- To increase the effectiveness of payment systems, some central banks are investigating the development of CBDCs, or digital equivalents of national currencies.

10. Charitable Donations:

 - The usage of cryptocurrencies in charity allows for transparent, fee-free contributions to worthy causes.

11. Cross-Border Trade:

- By offering an effective and borderless method of moving value, cryptocurrencies make cross-border trade easier.

12. Legal and Notary Services:

 - Smart contracts and unchangeable records are made possible by blockchain technology.

13. Micropayments:

 - Cryptocurrencies lessen the impact of transaction fees by enabling micropayments for little digital content and services.

14. Payments for the Freelance and Gig Economy:
- Cryptocurrency payments provide quicker settlement and lower fees for freelancers and gig workers.

15. Protect Against Economic Uncertainty:
 - Cryptocurrencies are utilized as a store of value and a safeguard against currency depreciation in areas where there is economic uncertainty.

16. Education and Certification:
- Academic credentials and certifications are issued and verified through the usage of blockchain technology.

Even if cryptocurrencies are becoming more and more popular in these regions, it's crucial to remember that things are always changing and that frameworks for regulations are being created to deal with the risks and difficulties that come with using them. The acceptance of cryptocurrencies in the future will rely on how these obstacles are overcome and how the technology develops and broadens its applications.

CONCLUSION

Through the pages of "The Cryptocurrency Investing Bible: How to Profitably and Safely Invest in Bitcoin, Ethereum, and Other Cryptocurrencies," we have traveled through the ever-changing landscape of digital assets. We have looked into the history of cryptocurrencies, including the creation of Bitcoin, Ethereum, and a plethora of other altcoins.

We've examined several investment techniques, talked about market mechanics, and examined blockchain technology. We've discussed the difficulties associated with taxation and legal compliance and underlined the need for risk assessment and safe storage. We've worked hard to provide you with a thorough handbook to help you

confidently and intelligently traverse the crypto
frontier as we go along.

As we come to the end of this voyage, it's important
to emphasize certain important learnings:

1. The Power of Knowledge:
 - Your best asset in the bitcoin market is
knowledge. Maintain a constant state of knowledge
about the projects you are interested in, the market,
and technology. Remain educated, but constantly
evaluate the sources of the information you come
across.

2. It's Critical to Manage Risk:
- Even though there is a lot of potential for profit in
the cryptocurrency market, risk management is
crucial. Make sure your portfolio is diversified,
evaluate your level of risk tolerance, and have a

well-defined plan for both short- and long-term investments.

3. There is no negotiation on due diligence:
- Make sure you've done your homework before contributing to any cryptocurrency initiative. Evaluate the community, the team, and the technology. Watch out for warning signs and possible frauds.

4. Safeguard Your Capital:
- Your cryptocurrency holdings' security is very important. Recognize the various wallet kinds, and safeguard your private keys by following best practices.

5. Remain Compliant:
 - Comply with local tax legislation and regulations. Maintaining compliance helps cryptocurrencies

become more widely accepted while also providing legal assurance.

6. Continue to Learn:

- The world of cryptocurrencies is always changing. Keep abreast of the most recent developments in technology and market trends. Digital finance has a bright future ahead of it, but it also demands flexibility.

7. Proceed With Caution:

- The cryptocurrency space is notorious for its unpredictability and volatility. Never invest more than you can afford to lose; always use caution. Remain sensible when investing because emotions such as fear and greed can sway judgments.

The cryptocurrency space has already had a significant influence on technology and finance. Its voyage is far from complete, and there are countless opportunities ahead of it. As you make your way through this terrain, keep in mind that your journey is only complete by your investigation, learning, and experience.

We hope that this tutorial has given you the groundwork and understanding required to get started on or carry on with, your Bitcoin investing journey. I hope your activities bring you prosperity, flexibility, and insight as the crypto frontier develops.

Recall that investing in the world of cryptocurrencies gives you the ability to influence how money, finance, and technology are developed. There's an opportunity to lead a financial revolution with countless opportunities.

We appreciate you coming along on your journey through "The Cryptocurrency Investing Bible," and

we wish you a bright and illuminating future in the
cryptocurrency space.

9 798866 533503